"Anyone facing challenges will benefit from the inspiration in *Connecting the Dots*. You'll get ideas to increase confidence and connect with others more effectively. It's a great read with lots of inspiring stories from Shirley and other global leaders."

Mark Sanborn
Leadership Strategist and author of
You Don't Need a Title to be a Leader

"Uplifting. Practical. Enthusiastic. Qualities of Shirley Taylor that exude from her and into this book. Wherever you are in your life and career journey, this book has tools that can shift your experience and lead you in the direction of greater confidence and growth. It's such an inspiration to read of Shirley's epic life journey across the world and in multiple industries, in leadership and within organizations.

Shirley shares her expertise in such an accessible and engaging way, with fabulously insightful questions and reflections along the way. *Connecting the Dots* is a professional and personal development book that brings with it reassurance that even when we cannot see the dots, sometimes until years later, they are connecting themselves."

Karen Jacobsen
The GPS Girl, International Speaker and Concert Performer

"We all have moments and people in our lives that shape us into the people we are today... dots on the timeline of our lives. Sharing right from the heart, Shirley from Sheffield shares her journey, her dots, and lessons learned. It's a great read that will inspire and motivate you to be your best self."

Chester Elton
The Apostle of Appreciation
Bestselling author of *Leading with Gratitude*,
The Carrot Principle and *All In*

"Shirley shares right from her heart in *Connecting the Dots*. In her book, you will find that none of us are self-made; we are all here because of people who touch us and are the essential dots in our lives. If you're looking for a push, a shove, some inspiration, and motivation, you're in the right place. This book will open your eyes to realize we can all achieve more than we know. What a great read!"

Andrea Limbach
CEO of RC Global Group

"If you dream big but are full of self-doubt, this book is in your hands for a reason. Shirley's story of how she stepped on and up the career ladder is inspirational. Her down-to-earth, practical advice will give you confidence and drive you to take action! A really great read!"

Peter Marshall, Managing Director
English Language Teaching Division, Oxford University Press

"Shirley's done it again. I've been an avid follower of her email and business writing books and training. Now we get to read the back story. In her training, Shirley shares from the heart, and she does just the same in *Connecting the Dots*. This is a great read especially for those at any kind of personal or career crossroads. Readers are sure to gain inspiration and advice that could lead to their future success!"

Carmelia Ng
Senior Manager, Talent & Organisational Development, Singapore

"*Connecting the Dots* is a delightful book from the ultimate business writing guru, Shirley Taylor. Packed with uplifting stories and powerful lessons from her extraordinary lifelong journey. It includes practical and positive insights from global leaders Shirley has befriended along the way. Buy this book and enjoy every page. *Connecting the Dots* will move you into action with enthusiasm and great joy!"

Ron Kaufman
New York Times bestselling author of *Uplifting Service*

"Shirley's sparkling personality jumps out from every page as she shares her journey and connects the dots in her life. If you've ever had a dream that seems just out of reach, this book will inspire you to reach for the stars and make them come true!"

Su-Yen Wong
Global Speaker and Board Director

"Shirley from Sheffield has shared from the depths of her soul in *Connecting the Dots*. If you're looking for some inspiration and motivation, you're in the right place. This book will open your eyes to realise we can all achieve more than we know by taking powerful lessons from past and future connections in your life."

Stephen Choo PhD
Managing Director
Digital Survey Research Insight Pty Ltd

"When you look at successful people, it sometimes seems easy for them. In *Connecting the Dots*, Shirley breaks down what it really takes to move forward in your career. Her passion makes every page come alive, and her writing reflects how she does everything – from the heart. A must read for those who want to move forward in their career."

Robin Speculand
Bestselling author and specialist in Strategy Implementation

"Shirley, it was such a great opportunity for me to see you present your keynote '*Connecting the Dots* to Grow Yourself and Your Business' in Singapore. It was a short presentation, but very thought-provoking and inspirational.

It's great to read more about your personal turning points in *Connecting the Dots to Inspire the Leader in You*. Your stories, lessons and ideas in this book will surely help many people to raise their game and elevate their success, even if they doubted themselves or had setbacks in the past. And your great sense of humour shines through in this book, as it did on stage! Such a great read!"

Nishant Kasibhatla
Peak Mental Performance Expert and
Guinness Record Holder in Memory (2011)

Shirley Taylor

Connecting *the* D●ts

TO INSPIRE
THE LEADER IN YOU

Reprinted 2021

Published by Marshall Cavendish Business
An imprint of Marshall Cavendish International

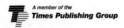
A member of the
Times Publishing Group

Other Marshall Cavendish Offices:
Marshall Cavendish Corporation, 800 Westchester Ave, Suite N-641, Rye Brook, NY 10573, USA • Marshall Cavendish International (Thailand) Co Ltd, 253 Asoke, 16th Floor, Sukhumvit 21 Road, Klongtoey Nua, Wattana, Bangkok 10110, Thailand • Marshall Cavendish (Malaysia) Sdn Bhd, Times Subang, Lot 46, Subang Hi-Tech Industrial Park, Batu Tiga, 40000 Shah Alam, Selangor Darul Ehsan, Malaysia

Marshall Cavendish is a registered trademark of Times Publishing Limited

National Library Board, Singapore Cataloguing in Publication Data

Name(s): Taylor, Shirley.
Title: Connecting the dots : to inspire the leader in you / Shirley Taylor.
Description: Singapore : Marshall Cavendish Business, [2020]
Identifier(s): OCN 1134854754 | ISBN 978-981-48-4152-8 (paperback)
Subject(s): LCSH: Success. | Leadership. | Self-actualization (Psychology)
Classification: DDC 650.1--dc23

Printed in Singapore

DEDICATION

To all the dots
I've met in my life so far,
and to all the dots
I have yet to meet.

CONTENTS

ACKNOWLEDGEMENTS

I have to start by acknowledging the person who first suggested the idea for this book several years ago, Tremaine Du Preez. It took me a while to get it going, but finally it's here. Thank you, Tremaine, for planting the seed.

Of course, every one of my 'dots' needs mentioning here, because without them there would be no dots to connect and therefore no book.

My first big dots are my Mum and Dad, who were always encouraging and supportive. I know they are beaming with love and pride as they watch over me. Rarely does a day go by that I don't say or do something that reminds me of one of them.

Linda Foster, my secretarial teacher, was such a great role model. Linda, after losing touch for almost 40 years, it was so good to reconnect with you recently. Thank you for inspiring me so many years ago, and I look forward to meeting up when I'm back in the UK.

I don't think I'd be writing this book at all if I hadn't met Pam Forrester in 1983 when she interviewed me for my first overseas post. She quickly became not just a close friend but a great supporter, mentor, and second mum. Sadly, Pam is no longer around, but I know she's always smiling down at me. I can't count the times I ask myself, "What would Pam say?"

In 1990, Peter Marshall and his colleague, David Buckland, visited the training centre where I worked in Singapore. They presented me with my first opportunity to enter the world of writing for a huge international publisher. Peter, I'm so glad we connected again recently after so many years. Thank you for setting me off on my writing journey. And what a journey it's been since that first book.

Leslie Lim, a lot of my subsequent books would never have happened without you always coming up with new ideas and suggestions. Thank you for your continuous encouragement, support and friendship.

David Lim, I know you joke that you say to a lot of people, "You'd make a good president one day," but saying it to me provided me with the push I needed to realise that I could become a leader. Thanks for planting the seed.

Scott Friedman, thank you for connecting me to so many fabulous people, for your hospitality when I've been in the States, and of course I'll never forget that special birthday party!

Nabil Doss, I learned so much from serving with you when you were President of the Global Speakers Federation. In particular, I learned what genuine, honest, authentic leadership is all about. You were an amazing role model and great friend.

My final dot is Heather Hansen. The day we met was one of those rare times when you meet someone who you feel you've known for years. With us, we felt sure it was over many previous lifetimes. Heather, thanks for your support and friendship, and for making me realise there was a way for me to move on while still leaving my legacy behind.

***

There are several others that I need to acknowledge too. First of all, a huge thanks to the many global leadership experts who contributed to this book. Thank you so much for your friendship, and for sharing your own personal turning points and the lessons you learned. I am always inspired talking to you, and I know that readers will learn a lot from your stories and insights.

Special thanks to Marianna Pascal for your friendship and support over many years. We were always a great sounding board for each other, and I learned a lot from you. In particular, I was grateful for your suggestion of starting each chapter in this book by looking into the reader's world. I hope you will feel that I did justice to this.

Big thanks to my assistant of many years, Rekha Sandiran, who also became a good friend. Rekha, you were a huge support, particularly during my last few years in Singapore. Thanks for being there to listen, support and provide some great ideas, as well as lots of fun and laughter.

Thanks also to Shirrey Grozen for taking good care of me, Cookie and Coco Chanel for over a decade. Shirrey, you have been a great support to us all. Thank you so much.

Big thanks to Nick French. From neighbour to good friend to trusted adviser and confidante. You've helped me so much in the past few years, and I know we'll share many more years of great friendship.

Barbara McNichol, it was great working with you as you edited my work. Your comments, edits and suggestions were so valuable.

Last but not least, a huge thanks to my friends at Marshall Cavendish International (Asia) in Singapore for your constant faith in me over many years and many books. In particular Lee Mei Lin, Publisher;

Anita Teo, Managing Editor; Mindy Pang, Marketing Manager; and Bernard Go, Creative Manager; plus of course all the other team members.

* * *

Finally, to you, the reader, thank you for choosing this book. As you turn the pages, I hope you find lots of stories that lift you up, motivate you, and inspire you to step forward or speak up. I hope you'll flip through these pages often and will always find something that helps you to unlock your true potential, and inspire the leader that I know is in you.

This is the book I wish I'd had the opportunity to read when I was 'just Shirley from Sheffield'. Because, believe me, if Shirley from Sheffield can do this, you can too!

Love and hugs

Shirley

 Join my Facebook group 'Shirley Taylor Connecting the Dots'. Share your stories of turning points and 'aha' moments from reading this book. Let's all help and encourage each other.

I am finishing writing this book at a time when there is much disruption in the whole world, not just in my life. As I write this, a few weeks before publication, many countries are just opening up after lockdown as a result of COVID-19. The future is uncertain for us all.

I am still in Singapore as I write this, and I don't know when I will be able to leave to head back to the UK. So there's a big question mark hanging over where and how my dots will connect for me in the future. But I am confident that they will, and I'm looking forward to meeting many new dots on my journey. As I write that last sentence, these famous words from Steve Jobs are ringing in my ear:

"You can't connect the dots looking forward; you can only connect them looking backwards. So you have to trust that the dots will somehow connect in your future."

– Steve Jobs

I hope you'll follow me and my journey as I continue to connect my dots. You'll find all my social media links on my website – www.shirleytaylor.com.

INTRODUCTION

"It is strange, but true, that the most important turning points of life often come at the most unexpected times and in the most unexpected ways."

– Napoleon Hill

I believe there's a leader inside each of us. Well, at least I do now. But I haven't always felt this way.

Growing up in Sheffield, England, I never felt like I was good enough. I was never the top of the class. I was always the last person to be picked in the sports teams. I often felt I was not as smart as the others in my class. I was just average. But I had great parents who loved me, and I had good friends. So, I was happy ... or was I?

As I grew up, others probably saw me as outgoing and confident, but how I felt inside was a different story. I was full of doubts and fears, worrying that I wasn't good enough, never feeling as pretty or as slim as my friends, being afraid to step up. I was frequently wondering, "Did I do or say the wrong thing?"

Does this sound familiar?

Whatever the reason you are reading this book, I'm glad you are, and I believe it's no coincidence. So, let me ask you a few questions:

It's no coincidence that you are reading this book right now.

Have you ever felt that you are not good enough?

Do you often doubt yourself or your decisions?

Do you feel you need a little push sometimes?

Do you ever dream of changing places with someone?

Do you wish you had more confidence when meeting new people?

Do you wish someone would give you just the right words of encouragement?

Have you felt stuck in your comfort zone with no courage to step out of it?

Have you seen a friend get promoted and wondered, "Why not me?"

Has something ever happened when you said "no", and you wish you'd had the confidence to say "yes"?

Trust me, I've been there. I've asked myself these questions and more. Many times. That's why I've written this book.

But even now a voice in my head is wondering, "Why on earth would people want to read your story?" and "Who do you think you are? You're just Shirley from Sheffield!"

Fortunately, I've now arrived at the point where I'm very proud to say, "I'm Shirley from Sheffield." But it's taken a long time – decades, in fact.

Not bad for Shirley from Sheffield who left school at 15 with no qualifications!

In this book, you'll read how Shirley from Sheffield ended up at the other side of the world in Singapore; how I was stunned when international publishers asked me to write my first book in 1991; how I was even more stunned when the same publishers asked me to write another book that has since sold over half a million copies and been translated into 17 languages; how I became chief examiner of a major UK examinations board; how I became founder and CEO of my own company providing training all across Asia; how joining a local speakers association helped me find a new passion and a global tribe of people I proudly call friends, many of whom are featured in this book; how that global tribe led me to becoming President of the Global Speakers Federation.

Not bad for Shirley from Sheffield who was always the last person chosen in the school's sports teams and left school at age 15 with no qualifications!

I can't take the credit for coming up with the idea to write this book, though. Years ago, a good friend of mine, Tremaine du Preez, said to me, "Shirley, you need to write a book called From Secretary to CEO. And if you don't write it, I will!" I laughed, but secretly I thought, "Wow! That's not a bad idea."

Several years later, after travelling the world for a year representing the Global Speakers Federation, my publishing friend Leslie Lim said to me, "Shirley, enough books on email and business writing. It's time for the leadership lessons you've learned – from being a secretary in Sheffield to becoming the President of the Global Speakers Federation."

"Enough books on business writing. It's time for the leadership lessons you've learned."

The common thread of lessons learned is proving even more important now, given the challenges of COVID-19.

As you'll learn through the pages of this book, when Leslie says things like this to me, I sit up and listen. This made me look back at all the significant turning points in my life and, in the process, recognise key lessons I'd learned – lessons that helped me grow both professionally and personally. In doing this, I was able to "connect the dots", as Steve Jobs famously said. Connecting the dots helped me uncover the common thread that runs through all my key turning points. And interestingly, this common thread is proving even more important now, given the challenges the whole human race faces with the COVID-19 pandemic.

In each chapter of this book, I develop the key lessons I learned by giving you practical tools to help you deal with all the questions you may have been asking. I also provide relevant questions so you can reflect on each topic and make notes. Writing down your thoughts can be highly liberating and energising. I strongly recommend you use writing to make the most of these interactive sections.

It may have been my imposter syndrome striking, but I realised you might enjoy some stories not only from me but from other people, too. So, I approached some global leadership experts I've been privileged to meet over the years. I was thrilled when every single person I asked agreed to be interviewed and featured in this book. I am immensely grateful for their contributions and friendship, and I know you will find their reflections, stories, and lessons inspiring.

Connecting my own dots through my writing journey has been a learning lesson in itself. It's May 2020 as I write this introduction. By this time, I had planned to be living in the UK starting a new life after living in Singapore for 18 years. But

> "The best-laid plans of mice and men often go awry."

no, I'm writing this while in lockdown in Singapore. As the old saying goes, "The best-laid plans of mice and men often go awry."

The global pandemic has affected all of us in many different ways. From my current vantage point in Singapore, I never thought I'd say this, but it looks like my stalled plans could be a blessing in disguise. Time will tell…

> "When life throws you lemons, you make lemonade."

Yes, life throws us curve balls sometimes. But there's an old saying that when life throws you lemons, you make lemonade. Right now, I'm enjoying the lemonade. I'm busier than I've ever been, and I hardly dare say it, but I'm also happier than I've been in a long time. Who would have thought it? Certainly not me! I won't spoil anything by saying more here. Instead, I'll update you on my Facebook group. You'll find the QR code at the bottom of this page.

As you turn the pages to read my stories and those of my friends, my hope is that you will find the courage and inspiration to unlock your true potential. I hope the lessons learned from my key turning points will help you navigate change, stay positive during challenges, and create new opportunities for growth and success.

This is the book I wish I could have read when I was Shirley in Sheffield feeling lost and looking for guidance. I hope it now provides guidance to you!

Wherever you are in life right now, thank you for trusting me to accompany you on your journey to connect the dots. Here's to your success!

Shirley Taylor

 Please join my Facebook group 'Shirley Taylor Connecting the Dots'. I'll be adding updates, interviews and other motivating content regularly. I'd also love to hear your 'aha' moments or turning points.

WHAT ARE YOU THIRSTY FOR?

Your passion will lead
to your purpose

1

*"Follow your passion.
It will lead to your purpose."*

– Oprah Winfrey

"Follow your passion." How many times have you heard this well-worn phrase? If only you knew what your passion was.

Finding and following your passion can be an issue for those just starting out in their careers. It's also an issue for many people who are stuck in jobs they don't enjoy.

Perhaps you have a steady job, you work hard, and you earn enough to provide for your family and yourself. It's routine and comfortable, but are you really fulfilled? Sometimes you may wonder if you've just accepted this as what's meant to be.

Or maybe you have some dreams about what you'd like to do, but you lack the confidence to do something about it.

Whatever is the case for you, you can be sure you are not alone.

But what if your passion is impatiently waiting for you to find it?

The world needs your passion. And when you find it, you can be sure that it will always guide you in the right direction.

✳✳✳

My early years

There was always lots of activity in my house as I grew up in Sheffield, England. Between my brother and me, we constantly had friends over. Mum would often joke, "Don't your friends have homes? They are always at ours!" We had lots of space to run around and play. Mum's baking was popular, and Dad loved to joke around with everyone. They always made our friends feel welcome.

No one in my family was shy of hard work. Mum started her career as a secretary until she got an opportunity to go into teaching. With no special qualifications, she became skilled at teaching shorthand and typewriting, and she loved it. She became a great role model for me.

Dad loved being outside with plants and flowers. He also had no qualifications, but he loved his job as head gardener in Sheffield Parks Department. I'd often take friends to the park where Dad was working, and we would get a free game of tennis or bowls. And because Dad was always joking, singing, and making up funny limericks, growing up was a lot of fun!

I was never academically talented, but I got by at school. I just wasn't interested in geography or history, and I wasn't good at mathematics. In junior school, I actually passed my Eleven Plus, which got me into high school. But although I enjoyed school and my friends, I didn't do well in a lot of subjects. But I did do very well in English, which I loved.

Growing up, I was always asking Mum about those funny squiggles when she wrote down notes. Those squiggles were actually Pitman's shorthand. I was happy when she started teaching me the basics of shorthand as well as touch typing.

At the start of my fourth year at high school (age 14-15), Mum and Dad had "the talk" with me about what I would do at the end of the year. In those days, parents could take their children out of school at the end of four years in high school. Mum and Dad both knew I cared more about shorthand and typing than mathematics and history. After a serious discussion, we decided I would leave school in the summer of 1971 and go straight to secretarial college for two years. I couldn't wait.

But the headmaster at my school had other plans. He was not at all happy when he brought in my family for a meeting. I remember him staring at my parents and saying, "Shirley needs to get some O levels. She must stay here for at least two more years so she gets some qualifications. If she doesn't do that, you'll really regret it!" Mum and Dad looked at me first and then at each other. They immediately stood their ground with the headmaster and removed me from school.

* * *

I'll never forget my first day at Granville College of Further Education starting a two-year secretarial course. Guess who got the role of being my Form Tutor? Yes, my Mum. When the department head told her she would take on this role for the new group, Mum asked him if it was a good idea. She didn't want to be seen as giving me any favouritism. Her boss told her, "Don't worry. The external results will tell their own story."

My fellow students quickly realised Mum wouldn't make me teacher's pet. Even in class, she insisted I call her "Miss" as the other students did. No favouritism for me! In fact, it was actually the contrary. If I told Mum I'd forgotten what she'd asked us to do for homework, I always got this answer: "Well, whose fault is that? Don't expect me to tell you!" After having to phone friends to ask several times, I soon learned my lesson.

I thrived at college. I made great friends and discovered I was good at something – in fact, lots of things. At the end of our second year, we had to face the dreaded external examinations. I studied hard and was so excited when I passed every examination with flying colours. At the prize-giving presentation that year, I was thrilled to receive the award for Student of the Year for having passed the most external qualifications. How proud my Mum and Dad were, and the department head was thrilled, too. I often wondered, "What would my old headmaster have thought about that?"

In July 1973, I immediately got a job as shorthand-typist at a large family firm in Sheffield. By working hard, I gained a reputation for producing high-quality work quickly. I enjoyed taking shorthand dictation from my bosses, typing quotations, memos and letters, and organising meetings. As a result, I was given more and more responsibility.

I also knew it was important to gain more qualifications, so I went to evening classes. Mum had earned a Pitman's certificate for 160 wpm shorthand, so I was keen to see if I could match or beat that. Eventually, I got a certificate for 170 wpm. In the first few years of working, I often took dictation from the chairman of the company. He would always try to push me by asking, "Shall I speak faster?" and then "Even faster?" Even today, rarely a day goes by that I don't write down notes using my shorthand.

* * *

One key event stands out from my days as a secretary. After taking dictation from my boss, I typed it as best I could. When I presented one important letter to him, he read it through, then looked at me, and said, "This is not what I said...." "Oh no," I thought, "I've done it wrong!" But then he smiled and quickly added,

Don't just do a good job. Do a great job!

"... but it's exactly what I wanted to say!" What a laugh we had. I took pride in putting myself in the reader's place and writing clear, concise messages that made sense and got the right response.

After being at this company a couple of years, I was promoted to be secretary to the financial director. When he eventually became the deputy managing director, I felt very proud to hold the role of his secretary until I left the company nine years later – in 1982.

"Leave your ego at the door every morning, and just do some truly great work. Few things will make you feel better than a job brilliantly done."

– Robin S. Sharma

Mum and Dad

Shirley with Mum and Dad.

LESSON:

Follow your passion. It will lead to your purpose.

What if...?

What if the school headmaster had won and I'd stayed on at school for two more years?

What if Mum and Dad agreed that I needed to get O and A levels?

What if I hadn't followed my passion?

What if I hadn't applied myself at college and achieved good results?

Mum and Dad knew what I was good at – and so did I. We also knew what I wasn't good at, and together we chose the right path for me. With their encouragement, I found my passion – not only for shorthand and typing, but for organising, administrative work, scheduling, meeting planning, and of course writing. But good was never enough for me; I always wanted to get better.

* * *

Leaving that company in 1982 was just the start of something big. After watching my Mum in action in the classroom, I knew I wanted to follow in her footsteps. Before long, it became obvious that my passion for secretarial work would lead me to my purpose – teaching and training. This ultimately led me to the first stage of a journey I could never have foreseen – one that took me far away from Sheffield and led to more passions and more purposes. You'll learn about them as you read through the pages of this book.

"If you can't figure out your purpose, figure out your passion. For your passion will lead you right into your purpose."

– T. D. Jakes

Moustafa Hamwi, aka Mr. Passion.

Reflections from Moustafa Hamwi

Moustafa was running a multimillion-dollar communication and entertainment business in Dubai and living what seemed to be a highly successful life. But he always felt like something was missing.

While his life looked super successful on the outside – like the kind of scenes you see in movies and rap videos – Moustafa did not feel fulfilled. The more glamorous his life had become, the emptier he felt.

One day in 2012, in pursuit of his passion and purpose, he bought a one-way ticket to India. During his journey there, Moustafa met a swami who had lived in caves for 13 years, where he led a life of solitude and meditation. He was now teaching wisdom-seekers in his ashram (temple) in a small village near the town of Manali in the Himalayas.

A swami is a spiritual teacher or guru who has set aside all worldly and materialistic ambitions to pursue a life of spiritual realisation and serve others in the same way.

Moustafa had many deep conversations with the swami, trying to get an answer about the purpose and meaning of everything in life. One day, the swami, contemplatively playing with his long beard, said, "Do you know what you are thirsty for? Because if you don't know what you are thirsty for, you cannot quench your thirst."

Moustafa told me, "Every time I tell this story, I feel teleported back to that moment. It is so vivid in my head and such an 'aha' moment for me. With that single statement from the swami, I realised I had

> When you ask the right question, you are more likely to find the right answer.

bought a one-way ticket to India seeking the answer, but I did not have the right question. I had no idea what I was thirsty for!"

Moustafa continued his journey across India, and one day he discovered he had a medical condition that experts labelled "non-curable". Determined to heal using natural means, he dedicated all his time and energy towards healing with the help of herbal medicine, healthy eating, and various kinds of meditation, including laughter and crying meditation.

Eventually, Moustafa recovered his health. However, this experience made him ask the question, "What if I did not recover and these were the last days of my life? Did my life really matter?"

He also asked himself three other questions, as if he really were in the last days of his life. I now encourage you to ask yourself the same questions:

1. Have I been fully engaged with life, or was I just a tourist?

2. Did I live a life that was meaningful to me, or did I just comply with other people's expectations?

3. Did I leave a legacy and an impact I am proud of?

Back in Dubai in 2013, Moustafa was invited to deliver an inspirational talk about his journey in India. A few months later, he bumped into a stranger who told him, "I attended your talk about your India journey. You changed my life!"

What a lightbulb moment this became for Moustafa! Finally, he knew what he was thirsty for! He was thirsty for being able to influence lives with his work and hearing more people say, "You changed my life." These words ultimately became his key performance indicator for knowing he was doing his job well.

From that moment on, Moustafa started speaking around the world about passion and its impact on our success in life and work. In the span of a few years, he earned the nickname "Mr. Passion", given to him by Professor Tony Buzan, inventor of Mind Mapping. Moustafa was also ranked as one of the top 100 coaches in the world by Dr. Marshall Goldsmith.

Here is how Mr. Passion defines passion: *"Consistently doing what you love, what you're good at, and what is of value to the world."*

 Reflections from Connecting the Dots. Watch exclusive interviews with all Shirley's guests.

> **"The secret to a truly passionate life is to trade your time, energy and efforts for what fulfils you the most."**
>
> **– Moustafa Hamwi**

Passion	Purpose
Life without passions can feel dull. Passions make life fun and exciting.	Life without purpose can feel aimless.
Passion is energy. It's what starts your engine.	Purpose is being useful, making a real difference in some way.
Passion is something so meaningful to you that you crave it.	Purpose is what you were put on this earth to do.
Passion is about emotions. It's an emotional spark that drives you forward.	Purpose is the reason you do what you do. It's the foundation on which your passion is built.
Passion can sometimes be selfish. When you pursue your passion, it's because you enjoy it and pursuing it feels good.	Purpose is never selfish. Your purpose could mean you have to put others first or put aside your own feelings for the sake of the greater good. But you won't mind doing so, because you know it's what you are meant to do.
Passion is ruled by emotions or feelings. It can often change on a whim.	Purpose is more focused. It might be *only one thing* that makes you feel fulfilled and complete.
Passion can come and go.	Purpose is forever, or perhaps until you've completed one purpose and find a new one.
Passion focuses on nouns. It's about what you love.	Purpose focuses on verbs because it brings in *action*. It completes you.

Passion, purpose and you

It's important to know the difference between your *passion* and your *purpose* because it can often help you get your life on the right track. When you know your purpose and give it all your time and energy, living your passion becomes even more focused and enjoyable. And having a good balance between passion and purpose will make your life worthwhile.

How do these descriptions of passion and purpose apply in your life?

The sweet spot is where your passion and purpose align. The ultimate life goal has to be following your passion while living out your purpose.

Does it always work to follow your passion?

"Follow your dreams" is the advice given by many people when it comes to choosing a job or career. But sometimes following your dreams – or your passion – can be risky. How many people move to Hollywood to chase their dream of being an actor only to find themselves in the unemployment line?

But what's the alternative? What happens if you ignore your dreams, your passion? This could lead you to putting your head down every day, slogging along, and doing dull, meaningless work that you don't enjoy, just to earn a salary.

I once saw an interview with comedian Jim Carrey in which he shared how his father had a talent for making people laugh but lived in fear of failure. His father chose the safe route of working in accounting, but when Carrey was just 12 years old, his father lost his job, putting his family in dire straits. Will you let fear rule you and take the safe route? Or will you follow your passion?

Questions to determine your passion

For many people beginning their careers, it can be impossible to identify your passion. It can also be tough for people who've been in the same job for years to figure it out. If you're having difficulty identifying your passion, answering these questions may help you.

1. **What would I do this year if I had no fear?**
    (from a Jana Stanfield song)
    What *would* you do this year if you had no fear? For decades, I wished I'd kept up with my piano lessons. I've decided that 2020 will be the year, *I will take piano lessons*. There, I said it. It's out there!

2. **What would you do if you could do anything?**
    Don't just say go on holiday or buy a big house. My friend Sue started attending art classes and found a huge passion. She's now selling her wonderful paintings and preparing for her own exhibition. I've decided that 2020 will be the year I join some kind of singing group.

3. **What do you really dislike doing?**
    List what you don't enjoy doing. Perhaps writing them down will make your true passion more apparent.

4   **Who do you really admire and why? What do they do that you respect?**
    I really respect my good friend Heather. She sets her mind on something and she does it. She's even a black belt at taekwondo.

5. **Ask your friends, family, or colleagues what they think you're good at.**

    Sometimes we don't know our own strengths. When you hear what they say, you might be surprised, so do give everything serious thought. My friends tell me I'm good at organising and going through all the fine details of a project.

6. **What are you good at but not great at?**

    Most people know they are okay at doing lots of things. Write these down and ponder over them. Could you weave any of these skills together in some way? Steve Jobs wasn't the world's greatest engineer, salesperson, designer, or businessman. Still, he was good enough at all of these to fuse them into something great – Apple.

7. **What did you love doing as a child?**

    Paint? Write stories? Recall what you enjoyed most during your childhood before you felt the pressure to study the right subjects or get a good job. Bringing back these memories can help you find your true passion now. I loved helping Mum to bake. I think I should dig out her recipe book, don't you?

8. **What new things could you create?**

    With every new thing you make, you're creating something to be passionate about. For example, my assistant Rekha loves Harry Potter, so she started designing her own wands, which she sells to family and friends.

9. **Imagine you are now 80 years old. What do you wish you had spent the last 20 to 30 years doing?**
   This exercise can be really cathartic and emotional. And it might just instigate a huge change in your life.

Don't expect a "eureka" moment from doing this exercise. These moments are rare. But inspiration could strike at any time once you pay attention to these important questions. Treat yourself by spending 15 minutes a day thinking about these questions and more. Inspiration or motivation often strikes as a result of a few small steps rather than one giant leap.

Two practices I strongly suggest are:

• **Meditation**
   Practising meditation helps you focus and think more clearly. It can clear your mind and determine what's going on within. It could even lead to you discovering your true passion.

• **Visualisation**
   Close your eyes and imagine it's early in the morning. The alarm goes off, and you jump out of bed feeling excited about the day. You have a spring in your step as you dress quickly, full of enthusiasm. The sun is shining brightly, you're smiling widely, and you take those first steps out of your house. Where are you going, and what kind of job follows from that amazing feeling?

"There is no passion to be
found playing small –
in settling for a life that
is less than the one you
are capable of living."

– Nelson Mandela

Your reflections

Here are this chapter's questions again with a space to answer them. If you wish, go back to the previous pages where they're explained. Give yourself quiet time to reflect and jot down your answers on paper.

1. What would you do this year if you had no fear?

2. What would you do if you could do anything?

3. What do you really dislike doing?

4. Who do you admire and why?

5. What do your friends, family, or colleagues think you are good at doing?

6. What are the things you are *good* at, but not *great* at.

7.   What did you love doing as a child?

8.   What new things could you create?

9.   Imagine you are now 80 years old. What do you wish you had spent the last 20 to 30 years doing?

"Since 80 per cent of your life is spent working, you should start your business around something that is a passion."

– Sir Richard Branson

COMFORT IS YOUR BIGGEST TRAP

Life begins at the end
of your comfort zone

2

"*You can't get to courage
without walking through
vulnerability.*"

– Brené Brown

Your boss has asked if you would take on a new project. It's bigger than anything you've ever tackled before. You're staring at her, your palms are sweating, your legs are shaking, and your heart is racing. Then you hear that voice in your head saying, "I can't do this." "I'm not prepared for this." "I'm going to fail, I know I will."

Does this sound familiar?

Stepping out of your comfort zone can mean different things to everyone. For you, it might be applying for a promotion at work. Or perhaps speaking in public. Maybe it's attending a networking event where you're sure you won't know anyone.

What happens to your body when you try something new? Do your palms start to sweat? Do you get stomach ache? Or do you just feel raw and vulnerable?

The truth is that every time you step out of your comfort zone, you will learn new things, you'll experience something exciting, and you can chalk up a tiny bit more self-confidence.

Because when you move past the fear, that's where the magic happens:

* * *

Working life leads to Super Secretary

I had been working as a secretary for several years, and I enjoyed going back to evening classes to study and gain higher-level qualifications. I knew I wanted to become a teacher, just like my Mum. However, unlike in Mum's day, if I were to teach in a college in the UK, I needed formal teaching qualifications.

The teacher training course I wanted to attend was in Huddersfield, about an hour's drive from Sheffield. To be accepted into the course, I needed either a degree or a qualification that was equivalent to a degree. I'd managed to get many qualifications in secretarial and business studies, but I'd never even considered that I was clever enough to get a degree.

Then I discovered that the LCCI Examinations Board Private Secretary's Diploma was considered "degree equivalent". If I had this qualification, I would be accepted into teacher training college in Huddersfield. Yes!

In 1981, I asked my boss if the company would pay for me to attend a course two nights a week so I could study for this qualification. He happily agreed.

Never be afraid to ask for something. If you don't ask, you'll never know!

The course teacher, Linda Foster, inspired me from day one. She was friendly and inspiring. As I watched her talking to the class, she had me hanging on every word. I watched the way she presented different topics, the way she engaged us and got us all involved in the learning experience. I studied hard and I didn't miss a lesson. I wanted to be a teacher just like Mrs. Foster.

One day, she told the class about a competition called Super Secretary 1981, organised by the Sheffield Junior Chamber of Commerce. Evidently, Chambers throughout the UK were holding these competitions, and Mrs. Foster encouraged all 18 students in our class to enter. I can still hear the collective groan when she mentioned this to us. But Mrs. Foster said it would help prepare us for the tough examinations to come. So all of us took her lead and entered the Super Secretary contest.

The competition involved typewriting, shorthand, and telephone technique tests, plus an interview. When the seven local finalists were announced, I found myself in this elite group. The awards ceremony was held at a local nightclub called Romeo and Juliet's.

What an exciting evening! My classmates came, Mrs. Foster too, my Mum and Dad, my friends and work colleagues, even my boss. When the results were announced, all seven finalists stood side by side on the stage, shaking in our shoes. First, they announced third place, then second. Finally, the winner was announced. Sheffield Super Secretary 1981 was... Shirley Taylor!

Yes, this young, sweet, innocent girl is me when I won the trophy for Super Secretary 1981 in Sheffield.

Wow! The audience went into an uproar. I remember hearing my Dad's voice shouting above all the others, "That's my girl!" The following day, my photograph appeared on the front page of our newspaper, *Sheffield Star*. I'll never forget it!

Over the next few exciting days, I was caught up with interviews and photos featuring my boss and me. Then Mrs. Foster broke the news that all local winners in various UK towns were automatically entered in a regional round of the competition. That meant I was now a candidate in the North of England Super Secretary competition.

This regional round involved more shorthand and typewriting tests plus a project that ended up being very detailed. I chose a project involving organising a company's annual dinner and dance, so I had to demonstrate I could plan every step of the process. I put as much effort into this hypothetical event as if I'd worked on it for my company. I wrote a narrative of every step, designed examples of every document – letters, memos, invitations, place cards, menus, and more – and I presented the results in plastic pockets placed in a beautiful binder. I remember it had a hard cover and a plastic pocket on the front, in which I put a title page including a colourful photo of a beautiful ballroom with round tables, and lots of people enjoying themselves.

> "If you want something you have never had, you must be willing to do something you have never done."
> – Thomas Jefferson

Of course, I didn't know any of the people in this regional round, but I knew we were all eager to attend the awards ceremony in Leeds. To my surprise, once again I was announced as the winner – Super Secretary 1981 North of England.

So imagine this. There's a winner from the north of England, a winner from the south, and yes, you guessed it, one from the west and one from the east. Four of us were now competing in the national final. This time there was nothing as basic as shorthand or typewriting tests. Instead, each of us had to prepare a 10-minute speech on a choice of topics. I'd never done anything like this before. But I was up for the challenge. I thoroughly prepared my topic on the future role and qualities of the executive secretary. I drafted, I rehearsed, and I redrafted some more.

All four regional finalists were invited to the national final in London, where we each presented our speech in front of our peers and the judges. Of course, I was very nervous, but I did my best, at times glancing at my notes on the lectern for support.

No fourth-, third-, or second-place winners were announced this time – just the main winner. "The United Kingdom's Super Secretary is..." And no, it wasn't me! But that was OK. I was a runner-up, along with the other two. We all felt extremely pleased and proud. My photo appeared again, not only in the Sheffield newspaper but in the national press!

I can't conclude this story without telling you about the prizes I won throughout this competition. At the local round in Sheffield, I won a portable electric typewriter (very exciting in those days). In the northern regional round, I won a briefcase with £200 worth of make-up, plus a holiday for two in Paris. I was happy and proud, as were my parents. Especially proud was Linda Foster, who had coached me along the way.

What one thing did this competition give me more than anything else? It gave me more self-confidence.

As I mentioned earlier, I wasn't the brightest kid in school. Being the last one chosen for team sports didn't do much for my confidence. I would never have put myself forward for anything. So with this competition, the fact that Mrs.

When was the last time you took a leap of faith and did something for the first time?

Foster saw something in me and encouraged me at every step of the way, well, that boosted my confidence in a huge way. Winning the competition and then being a runner-up in the national final went way beyond my wildest dreams.

* * *

After the excitement of the competition died down, my classmates and I threw ourselves into working hard on the course. At the end of the year, I passed every examination with flying colours. I knew the next stage of my life was confirmed. Attaining the LCCI Private Secretary's Diploma was exactly what I needed to be accepted into a one-year full-time teacher training course in Huddersfield.

When I told my boss the good news about passing my exams, I jokingly said, "Thanks so much for paying for my course. Oh, and by the way, I resign!" He laughed, but he knew that day would come. I had told him all about my aspirations to be a teacher, and he gave me not only his blessing but the most fabulous testimonial I could have hoped for. These sentences particularly made my heart sing: "Shirley always takes pride in her work and is meticulous in everything she does. I could not recommend her more highly."

***

My experience in this competition and in this course was my first step towards realising that people can achieve much more than they often think or believe. I know if Linda Foster hadn't encouraged me to enter the competition, my life may have taken a different turn. But going through this process, feeling supported, being encouraged, as well as pushing myself, increased my confidence so much.

Looking back, I realise this also made me more willing to take risks in the future – and take risks I did. Back in 1981, I could never have imagined the depth of my risk-taking in the years that followed.

"Only those who risk going too
far can possibly find out how
far it's possible to go."

– T.S. Eliot

Linda Foster

Linda in 1981   Shirley and Linda catch up on Zoom in 2020

LESSON:

Life begins at the end of your comfort zone.

What if...?

What if I'd never taken that evening course?

What if I'd not taken up the challenge of entering the Super Secretary competition?

What if my teacher Linda Foster had not encouraged me?

What if I hadn't put a lot of hard work and effort into the competition?

Let's imagine I had not attended that course, but I'd seen the competition advertised in the local newspaper. Would I have entered? Not likely! Why? Because sometimes we need a shove. And Mrs. Foster's encouragement helped all of us a lot. She believed in us, she pushed us, and we supported each other. And now, 39 years later, I still feel grateful for that!

Rarely will others push us, so we need to push ourselves!

In entering that competition, I had stepped out of my comfort zone, and I soon realised that, when I do that, great things can happen. A whole new set of possibilities open up. They may feel scary at first. Even now, I often wonder, "Can I do this?" But once I make a commitment and start focusing, I become passionate about it, and my confidence expands.

Reflections from Nishant Kasibhatla

In 2006, Nishant Kasibhatla was a freelance corporate trainer in New Delhi, India, teaching memory skills. He had plenty of work, so everything may have *looked* great to an outsider, but Nishant didn't *feel* great. He kept sensing something wasn't right. He wasn't fulfilled.

Nishant Kasibhatla, Guinness World Record Holder, Grand Master of Memory

One day, Nishant was watching a television interview with Lakshmi Niwas Mittal, a billionaire who was the richest man in India at the time. The interviewer asked, "What's your advice for young entrepreneurs to be more successful?" Very casually, Lakshmi answered, "Challenge your comfort zone."

> "Whenever you feel uncomfortable, instead of retreating back into your old comfort zone, pat yourself on the back and say, 'I must be growing,' and continue moving forward."
>
> – T. Harv Eker

Nishant had heard this phrase a million times before, but this came at a pivotal moment. He started thinking, "Holy moly! This guy started from humble beginnings and went on to become the richest guy in India. Of all the advice he could have given viewers that day, he challenged us to break out of our comfort zones."

From that moment, everything started changing for Nishant.

Wondering if he had heard this message for a reason, Nishant shared the story with his wife, Rakhi, asking, "Should we carry on here in New Delhi, or should we challenge our comfort zones? What do you think about starting afresh in a new country where we don't know anyone?"

Later that year, they left the only country they'd ever known and moved to Singapore. They chose Singapore because, at the time, it seemed to be the easiest place for them to set up a business. The hub of Southeast Asia, it was also a melting pot of different nationalities.

> "Nothing happens unless something is moved."
> – Albert Einstein

Of course, it wasn't easy at first, and after two months, nothing was working. They had moved from India to one of the most expensive countries in the world, and they found they were burning through their money like crazy. Nishant and Rakhi sat down to discuss their situation. This time, instead of focusing on the facts (no money, no work, new country, new culture, no contacts), they started looking at their goals and dreams. Once they listed them on paper, they discussed how they could achieve them. This proved to be a game-changer.

Nishant started attending networking events. He and his wife both made countless cold calls, offering free presentations anywhere and everywhere. People loved what he did, and pretty soon engagements were coming in.

Nishant and Rakhi have since created an amazing life in Singapore, raising their two sons and working together in their hugely successful business running public events for children and adults. Nishant is also a popular professional speaker, delivering keynotes to audiences as big as 5,000 people, and conducting training programmes on mindset, learning, focus, speed reading, motivation, and success.

Nishant is glad he chose to challenge his own comfort zone. What makes the difference? He says it's not about *knowledge* itself; everyone can attain knowledge. Rather, it's about *what we do* with that knowledge that counts. Often that means shifting our mindset, because that's what determines if we actually apply our knowledge to improve our life.

Changing his mindset is the shift that helped Nishant challenge his comfort zone, and he now helps others to do exactly the same.

Reflections from Connecting the Dots.
Watch exclusive interviews with all
Shirley's guests.

> "I am constantly challenging myself to do new things, take risks and challenges. I encourage others to do the same. That's the way we grow."
>
> – Nishant Kasibhatla

You and your comfort zone

Check out the words inside the comfort zone circle here. Do they look familiar? Do any of them describe you or your feelings about your situation right now?

Look at what exists outside the comfort zone. Isn't it worth taking that leap right now?

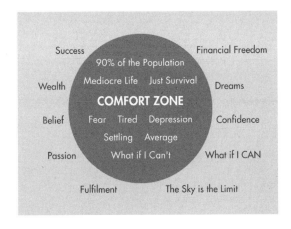

The change cycle

When you take a risk of any kind – do anything different, try something new, take on a challenge – or when someone challenges you, the result is always change. And change can be scary. For some people, even taking a different route to drive to work might bring on a panic attack.

In my training programmes, I share a simple but effective way of discussing what happens with change of any kind. Here's the diagram and the flow I share:

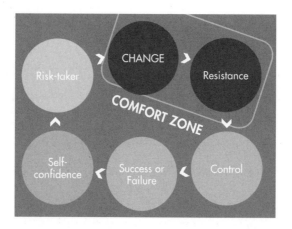

Go through this process step by step, and then examine how you might feel at each step:

1. Change

Here's how you might feel here: *Nervous, uneasy, tense.*

So here you are facing a situation when you are considering doing something different. For me, I had

> "In any given moment we have two options: to step forward into growth or step back into safety."
> – Abraham Maslow

the opportunity to enter a competition. You may be asked to take on a new project at work, or consider a new job. Basically, you get or look for an opportunity to do something that would take you out of your comfort zone.

2. Resistance
Here's how you might feel here: *Negative, fearful, hesitant.*

As you stand on the edge of your comfort zone, the first feeling you'll get is resistance as you wonder: "Can I do this?" "Do I step out?" "What will happen if I step out?"

It's normal to feel resistance. Stepping out of your comfort zone seems scary. You will feel nervous. You will wonder, "Is this a good idea or not?" "Do I really want to do this?" "Can I really do this?"

If you stay in your comfort zone too long, it will become very uncomfortable. Why? Because everyone else will have moved out!

When you put together step 1 and step 2, this section describes your comfort zone – your "safe place" or your "comfortable place". And this is where you could stay if you decide to do so. It's where many people decide to stay.

3. Control
Here's how you might feel here: *Apprehensive, excited, energised.*

Here comes the scariest part – the part when you take control. Scary, yes, but exciting at the same time. You decide, "Yes! I'm going to do this." You start making preparations, you draft a plan. It feels really good. Scary, but good. Moving forward, you start your new project, the new job, riding a bike, whatever it is. You take control, and you do it to the best of your abilities.

4. Success or Failure

Here's how you might feel here: *Creative, productive, focused.*

Here's the result. I like to think of this step as *success* rather than *failure*, because no matter what the result, you have succeeded in stepping out of your comfort zone. You put your mind to your new project, and you completed it. Isn't that success in itself? Whatever the result, to my mind, you've been successful because you stepped out of your comfort zone. And I truly believe that, more often than not, if you put 100% effort into it, this step will be a huge success!

5. Self-confidence

Here's how you might feel here: *Invigorated, positive, motivated.*

Here comes the truly wonderful part. Every time you do something new or different, your confidence is bound to increase. What a wonderful feeling! You've done it. Well done! You may get accolades or rewards in other ways. But even if you don't, you can count on this: Every time you do something different, your confidence will increase.

6. Risk-taker

Here's how you might feel here: *Inspired, stimulated, driven.*

In the Super Secretary competition, by winning the local Sheffield round, I felt confident to take the risk of competing in the northern regional round. And because others had seen potential in me, it gave me a boost to work even harder in the next round. This will be the same with you. As you take on new things and do more different things, you will become a risk-taker. And guess what? This amazing feeling is contagious. It's going to make you want to start all over again and try something else, then something else. Heck! I'm now here writing my 16th book. Who would have believed it? Certainly not Shirley from Sheffield! Bring on number 17, that's what I say!

> ## "The risk of breaking out of your comfort zone is not nearly as bad as the risk of staying in it your whole life."
>
> – Unknown

10 things you can do now to step out of your comfort zone

1. Smile at everyone you pass in the street.

2. Try something new from the menu at lunch time.

3. Ask to take on a project at work that makes you feel a little nervous.

4. Start a conversation with a colleague you don't normally speak with.

5. Write a sweet note for a loved one and hide it somewhere that's easily found.

6. Be kind to everyone, be grateful, smile, and always say, "Thank you."

7. Do something spontaneous, either on your own or with friends.

8. Do something different with friends on the weekend.

9. Ask a boss or a partner for something you want.

10. Reach out to seemingly inaccessible people you admire and tell them how they impacted your life.

"Be aware that things are going to change. We have to get into the uncomfortable zone before we can move into the growth zone."

– Nishant Kasibhatla

Your reflections

Now it's your turn to reflect on some important questions. Answering these questions may help you get unstuck if you've been stuck. It may give you an "aha moment" where you recognise what's been holding you back. It may help you realise that you can and you will move out of your comfort zone right now!

1. When was the last time you did something outside your comfort zone?

2. How did you feel when you did that? Describe your feelings.

3. Did you see any positive results when you stepped out of your comfort zone?

4   Have you ever said no to doing something because of fear or nerves?

5. What would you do today if you had no fear?

6. What's one thing you will do today to step out of your comfort zone?

"Move out of your comfort zone. You can only grow if you are willing to feel awkward and uncomfortable when trying something new."

– Brian Tracy

NO ONE SAID LIFE WOULD BE EASY

We grow when
we face challenges

3

"Life's challenges are not
supposed to paralyze you;
they're supposed to help you
discover who you are."

– Bernice Johnson Reagon

Life is full of challenges. Some people are able to face any challenge confidently, while others struggle. Others actually seek out challenges. What about you?

Do you avoid challenging situations, or even run away from them? Do you get frustrated when faced with a challenge, so you put it off? Or do you just confront it head on?

The thing is, it's impossible to achieve anything in life without some stress or torment. It's inevitable.

If you want to lose some unwanted pounds, you must face the challenge of changing your lifestyle and eating habits.

If you want a better job, you must face the challenge of job searching, interviews, or maybe training for something new.

If you want to stop smoking or beat an addiction, you must face the challenge of facing doctors and therapy.

Rarely can anything be accomplished without hard work, and that often means feeling uncomfortable. But after the pain or stress of the challenge, there is the joy and pleasure of coming out the other end a better person for it.

* * *

Goodbye Sheffield, Hello Singapore

My year at Huddersfield teacher training college was everything I'd dreamed and more. To my great surprise, I even loved studying psychology and sociology. I was motivated reading about Pavlov and his dog, and I really enjoyed learning all the techniques and tools for teaching.

But goodness, what an example of stepping out of my comfort zone! Almost daily, we were doing new things that stretched us, that challenged us.

Working in local colleges to do teaching practice was nerve-wracking but also useful and rewarding. Again, it boosted my confidence, and I quickly realised I'd found my new niche. I loved the course and again I felt so inspired by the teachers.

If it doesn't challenge you, it doesn't change you.

At the end of our graduation year, 1983, my friends and I looked through the newspapers for jobs. One that appealed to me was in a West Midlands town called, believe it or not, Shirley. The interview went well, and I received a letter offering me the job. However, something kept bothering me. When I saw an advertisement with the headline "Teacher wanted to teach on LCCI Private Secretary's Course", well, this was more like it! But the next line completely floored me: "...in Singapore"! "Where's Singapore?" I asked my friends. One said, "It's in China." Another said, "No, it's in Hong Kong." None of us had any idea. (You'll recall that I didn't pay much attention in my school geography classes.) I went to the college library and searched in the atlas, and there it was – a little red dot marked Singapore. It was on the other side of the world!

For a girl who'd grown up in Sheffield and hadn't travelled much further than Bridlington for annual family holidays, taking a job on the other side of the world was very daunting.

> **Encourage your children, because you have no idea what they are truly capable of.**

When I went back home that weekend, I waited patiently to choose my moment to speak to my parents about this advertisement. Many parents would have said, "No, stay here. Take the job in the Midlands." Or "Don't leave us. Get a job here." But no, Mum and Dad looked at each other and, almost in unison, said, "You go for it, Shirley."

My parents supported me every step of the way. Before the weekend was over, my application and résumé were in the mail to the LCCI Examinations Board, who were advertising and interviewing in London on behalf of the Singapore school.

* * *

On the day of my interview, I had a long journey from Sheffield to London and the LCCI headquarters. In the interview room, two people were sitting behind the table – a gentleman on the right, and a lady on the left who introduced herself as Pamela Forrester. Although I don't remember the questions they asked me, one incident towards the end of the interview stuck with me. The gentleman wrote a note and passed it to Miss Forrester. She smiled, wrote on it, and passed it back. (You'll find out later what the note said.) Then they asked me to sit outside for a few minutes. I sat there nervously, only to be invited in again and offered the job. I found out later that I had been scheduled at the end of the day because they had already determined I was the most promising candidate for the job.

I accepted the job right there on the spot.

* * *

In August 1983, my parents said goodbye to me at the airport, and I boarded what was only my second plane ever. This was not a two-hour holiday trip to Spain though. I was headed to a new country and a new life on the other side of the world. For Shirley from Sheffield, life would never be the same again.

My story of arriving at Singapore Changi Airport is one that I've told many times in training programmes and presentations. And no doubt I will tell it many more times. My Singaporean boss (Rose) and her colleague (Joon) came to the airport to meet me. I sat in the back seat of their car as they drove to the house where I would stay. I chattered away the whole car ride, pointing at the boats and trees and talking about the long plane ride. I babbled on about anything and everything. And neither of the two women said anything. Not a word.

It was six months later when I learned why. Pamela Forrester came to Singapore on one of her annual visits to help guide the teachers and advise the students. That's when Pamela told me that, as soon as Rose got home after dropping me off at my new home, she phoned Pam in the UK. The conversation went like this:

Pamela: "Oh hello, Rose, has Shirley arrived safely?"

Rose: "Yes, she's arrived, but we don't understand a word she says. We are sending her home on the first plane tomorrow."

Pamela: "Oh don't worry, dear, I'm sure she'll soon realise that she needs to make some changes. Give her a chance, please."

Remember, no one told me this until Pamela came to Singapore six months later.

The day after I arrived, I went down to the school to meet Rose, Joon, and the other teachers. What a culture shock meeting my new colleagues, all of them Singaporean, Chinese, Malay, Indian, or Indonesian. As I was introduced to everyone, I soon realised that every time I spoke, staring back at me was the same blank face: head tilted a little, eyes squinting, eyebrows raised, mouth slightly agape. It didn't take me long to realise why. They didn't understand my Sheffield accent!

From then on, I had to repeat things, sometimes many times, and clarify what I was saying. You see, they knew Pamela from the south of England who spoke almost the Queen's English, which is rather posh. In the north of England, we speak, well, quite differently. One other expatriate, Candice, had been teaching at the school for two years. As she was from Cheshire, Candice had a different accent from mine and very similar to Pamela's. When my new colleagues met Shirley from Sheffield, they had a shock and quickly discovered not all English people speak the same!

*** ***

It wasn't easy adjusting to my new life in Singapore, but I knew that my accent was the first thing I had to change. One day I was teaching a class and telling the students about the different foods I'd been eating since I arrived. I said, "Last night, my friends took me out, and it was the first time I'd eaten duck." Many students stared at me looking shocked, and one girl asked loudly, "You ate a *dog*?" I quickly realised that, with my accent, *duck* sounded like *dog* to them! I had to change the way I said other words too, such as *bus, cup, mug, love, up, under* and anything else where I'd been using a deep Yorkshire "u" all my life!

If things are not working as well as they could be, it's time to reinvent yourself.

We did have some fun with my accent, but the bottom line was this: I had to clarify some of my words in every conversation. Before long, I took time to pronounce everything more clearly, placing a particular emphasis on the beginnings and endings. And I learned the importance of slowing down my speech.

Those first few months in Singapore provided a steep learning curve for me. On top of my language difficulties, I had the shock of living very close to the equator, with a humid climate of around 28 degrees Centigrade most of the year. I'd never known any heat like that in my life. The college where I worked was in the middle of Orchard Road in the centre of the city. Orchard Road was full of big shopping malls and tall buildings, as well as loads of tall trees that provided useful shade as we walked around. Little did I know how those trees would hold such meaning for me as I continued my Singapore journey.

* * *

After a few months in my new home, I realised I'd been feeling depressed for a while. I was missing home, the UK, my family and friends. Did I make a dreadful mistake? Should I have accepted the job in the Midlands instead?

Not able to shake off this depression, I went to see my doctor, a nice Chinese man. After tearfully telling him my story, he sat back and smiled at me. To my surprise, he asked me questions about the trees along Orchard Road. The conversation went like this:

Dr. Wong: "Have you seen all the huge trees on Orchard Road, Shirley?"

Me (puzzled):   "Er, yes."

Dr. Wong: "Do you think those trees began their life there, or do you think they began life somewhere else?"

Me (still puzzled): "Well, I suppose they were originally planted somewhere else when they were baby trees."

Dr. Wong: "And then what?"

Me: "Well, I guess when they started growing, they were brought to Orchard Road and replanted."

Dr. Wong: "And what do you think happened, Shirley, when those trees were first replanted on Orchard Road?"

Me: "Well, I guess they might not have been very happy, so they could have wilted and died a little at first."

Dr. Wong: "And then what happened?"

Me: (I started to smile, realising where the doctor was going, and I knew his analogy made perfect sense to me.) "I imagine they soon started putting down roots and feeling more comfortable in their new surroundings. Then eventually they started to grow into the beautiful big trees they are today."

Dr. Wong: "Exactly, Shirley. Give it time. Everything new takes time to get used to. Even a new pair of shoes can pinch a little until you wear them in."

This talk with Dr. Wong helped me to put everything into perspective. Pamela's visit to Singapore soon after helped even more. I didn't realise it then, but she became one special lady who would have a significant effect on my life for the rest of her days.

Pam had taken a chance on me by offering me this job. I'd stepped right out of my comfort zone by moving to the other side of the world into an unknown culture.

"Storms make trees take deeper roots."

– Dolly Parton

Someone who was a huge support to me during my initiation to Singapore was Candice, my predecessor at the training school where I worked. Candice and I became quick friends, enjoying coffee shop lunches in the middle of training days, high teas at super hotels, and a glass of wine (or two) over dinner.

Our friendship has continued over time and distance. Candice is now happier than ever, living back in Cheshire, and I've visited her there many times.

When I visited UK not too long ago, she said, "OK if you can't come up to me, I'm coming down to you." Candice treated me to a wonderful stay at 'her club' in London, and we had the best couple of days catching up. Candice is definitely another 'dot' in my journey of life.

Having fun with Candice in London, 2019

Pam Forrester

Shirley and Pam.

LESSON:

We don't grow
when things are easy.
We grow when we
face challenges.

What if...?

What if I'd decided to take the job in the West Midlands instead?

What if Pam had been concerned about the note from her colleague during my interview?

What if I didn't have Pamela for support and guidance?

What if I hadn't been able to change my accent when I arrived in Singapore?

What if I'd just thrown in the towel and gone home when I got depressed?

Pam followed through by encouraging me at every step of the way over those first two years in Singapore and beyond. She really took me under her wing. She supported me in letters, in phone conversations, and on her annual visits to Singapore as a mentor for the principal and teachers. Pam became my fairy godmother, my best friend, my mentor, my second mum. She was someone I could always reach out to for advice at any time.

Pam regularly dried my tears, picked up my spirits, and helped me to become more resilient. I wouldn't be anywhere close to where I am today if it wasn't for the fateful day that I met Pam Forrester.

Oh yes, and remember I mentioned the note that the gentleman who interviewed me with Pam passed to her during my interview? Pam later told me that it said, "She's perfect. But will they understand her accent?" Pam wrote on it, "She'll be fine!"

"If it doesn't challenge you
it doesn't change you."

– Fred DeVito

Reflections from Dali Schonfelder

When I saw Dali Schonfelder speak at an international speakers convention in Singapore in 2019, I knew from her first sentence that I wanted to know more about her. Those first words were, "Let the way you live be the way you give."

Dali Schonfelder, young entrepreneur and motivational speaker, with her brother, Finn.

Every year, Dali Schonfelder and her family travelled from their home in Holland to a rural village in the outskirts of Mumbai, India. Dali and her brother Finn made friends with children in the playgrounds, and India soon became their second home.

On their annual visit when Dali was just 13, she was shocked to find that her friends were no longer attending school because at the age of 12, the government stops paying for uniforms. If they cannot afford the mandatory uniform, students are forbidden to attend school and can no longer receive an education. Of course, this causes enormous school dropout levels, especially within the poor communities.

Wanting to do something to help her friends, Dali and Finn founded Nalu, a clothing line that gives one school uniform with the sale of every four products.

Dali told me, "I remember giving my very first school uniform to a girl called Pretty, who was almost 13, so she was about to leave school. When I gave Pretty her school uniform, we just looked into each other's eyes, two young girls, and at that moment I knew Nalu was going to work. Pretty rushed to the bathroom to slip into her new school uniform, then as she walked back across the red dusty school grounds, she was so happy and full of pride that she looked five centimetres taller. Since then, Pretty has graduated from high school and is now in university studying to become a teacher so she can pay it forward."

In 2015, Nalu opened their first store in Bali. They employ local women as tailors to make the uniforms, ensuring the full cycle of sustainability within the community they give. The impact Nalu has made has been tremendous. Not only has enrolment doubled, but academic performance has improved, with grades going up by an average of 22%. On top of this, girls are staying in school longer, which has led to a huge decrease in teenage pregnancy.

But of course, it hasn't all been plain sailing. When Dali was 15 and so much was already happening with Nalu, she knew that to get to the next level she needed someone who could mentor her. Donna Karan had always been one of her idols, so Dali sent her an email. Imagine her surprise when Dali received a reply asking her to attend a meeting at her DKNY store Urban Zen in New York.

Dali told me, "Imagine, I'm 15 and my idol wants to meet me, and my parents allowed me to fly halfway across the world to New York. But when I arrived at her store, she had cancelled the meeting. I was devastated."

Never one to give up at the first hurdle, Dali asked to meet the CEO, and she told him all about Nalu. The CEO said to her, "Why not make some t-shirts that we can sell in our store in New York? We'll need them by May." A very excited Dali flew back to Bali, made all the t-shirts, and then emailed him to say they were ready. No reply. She emailed again. No reply to any of her 15 emails. As May was approaching, Dali asked her mum and dad if she could fly to New York to hand-deliver the shirts. Of course, they said "yes".

Dali walked into Urban Zen, armed with a big bag full of Nalu t-shirts, and can you guess who just happened to be there? Yes, Donna Karan! She opened up her arms to welcome Dali, they became great friends, and Donna Karan is still mentoring Dali to this day.

Dali told me, "I always tell people not to let one thing stop you from doing what you really want to do. If I had stopped after not receiving a reply to my emails, this and so much more would never have happened."

Since then, Nalu has grown from strength to strength. Nalu has given over 4 million days of school to children all over the world. As at the time of publication of this book, they have given over 12,000 uniforms to children across India, Kenya and Indonesia, and have another 4,000 scheduled this year. Their goal is to scale to give 2,000 uniforms per month by 2025. In 2017 they launched the Nalu Academy, an online school teaching and empowering youths through social entrepreneurship.

 Reflections from Connecting the Dots. Watch exclusive interviews with all Shirley's guests.

"**If you say no to opportunities or take no for an answer, your life will be so different and you won't be able to impact as many people as you want. There are so many problems in the world. Find something you're passionate about and find a solution to them. Go for what you want, because if you go the extra mile, there won't be so much traffic along the way.**"

– Dali Schonfelder

Dali now speaks on international stages. She has shared her story at the United Nations, and she was selected out of thousands of applicants for the Global Teen Leader of the Year 2017. At the young age of 19, Dali is such an inspiration to many. She is passionate about inspiring the younger generation to take action on the causes they believe in so they can play their part to help make a better tomorrow.

Why women resist change

I was honoured to be able to interview women's leadership expert Sally Helgesen when I hosted my inaugural online summit, the Future Leaders Summit. You can still benefit from this at www.futureleaderssummit.com.

In our interview, Sally shared distinct differences between the way men and women deal with change. I'm delighted that Sally allowed me to share a summary of our discussion in this chapter.

When men get feedback about something they need to change, they often get angry or blame the person giving them the feedback. By contrast, women tend to take the feedback to heart and may start to feel bad about it. And when you feel bad, you're more likely to become paralysed, confused, and avoid asking for help.

Neither approach is very high-functioning, but the way women resist change makes them feel worse. One way that women can move themselves forward when they get feedback is to turn it into a positive and a win for them.

It's important to recognise when feedback is not accurate or not particularly informed.

> **Feeling bad is not a behaviour that helps you succeed. It's a form of resistance.**

If that's the case, or you perceive it is not well intended, just say "Thank you" and move on.

Blind spots that get in women's way

Sally's work identifies some classic blind spots:

1. **A reluctance to claim their achievements.** When someone says, "Good job," women often deflect and say something like, "Oh, it was my team members; I couldn't have done it without them." Why not graciously say, "Thank you"?

2. **Expecting others to spontaneously notice and value their contributions** without having to draw attention to themselves or articulate it. The trouble is, in our busy work world, people often don't take notice.

3. **Women are often expected to be unfailingly generous and nurturing, and they fear being accused of arrogance if they respond in a direct way.** Being overly attentive to expectations in an effort to please can make it difficult for you to hold others to account or assert important boundaries.

4. **Women often get caught in a kind of loyalty trap,** afraid of positioning themselves to move on for fear of disappointing their boss or team. The result? You may put your job before your career.

5. **Another common trap for women is perfectionism,** feeling they need to be precise and correct in everything, and that if they make mistakes they're failures. This kind of "either/or" mindset makes it difficult to take the kind of measured risks required to claim effective leadership.

6. **Women tend to believe they need to become an absolute expert** to position themselves for the next job. However, being perfect for the job you currently have only proves you are perfect for *that* job. This thinking can keep you stuck.

> Don't start a sentence with "I'm sorry...". This is minimising in advance.

7. **Young women in particular tend to minimise.** They do this either verbally or in their body language by shrinking themselves or saying things such as "This will only take a second" as if they're wasting the other person's time.

Sally's three legs of expertise

Sally believes women should build their careers on these three "legs":

1. Do a good job; become known for your expertise.

2. Be visible; become known for your accomplishments and achievements.

3. Build a wide, strong network of relationships you can leverage.

Women need to be comfortable asking what people think of the job they're doing and getting advice. They also need to look at how they're building their network and their confidence while assessing which path will lead them to where they want to go.

Building a broad but strategic network is essential. Think of it in terms of "This is the kind of contribution I would like to make in my job or in my career." Find out who could be helpful and how you could get to know them. Then engage them and ask how you could also be of service to them.

Getting others to invest in your career will strengthen you and give you more support.

Where do you start?

After identifying your blind spots, Sally suggests you should not try to change everything at once. Start with the behaviour that's easiest to address, and then enlist people to help you.

For example, to be more concise in your presentations, ask a colleague to watch you and provide feedback. Or ask someone who's concise in her presentations if she has tips for you. This engages people in your development and gets you comfortable with all kinds of feedback. It also advertises to others that you're making positive changes. Research shows that people who engage others to help them are most successful at making long-term positive behavioural changes.

Peer coaching can also have great value. You don't have to wait until your organisation has a big budget to hire a professional to work with you. Instead, start right away with a friend or colleague. Let your peer coach know what you want to work on and ask her to hold you accountable. Then do the same for her.

Your reflections

1. What opportunities or invitations have you said "no" to, when really you wish you'd said "yes"?

2. When have you been in a position where you needed help, but you were too proud to reach out and ask someone?

3. If someone tells you that you did a great job, what do you normally say? How could you change this in future?

4. Look back at the list of blind spots. Can you identify some of yours?

5. Who could you buddy up with at work to be peer coaches? How will you help keep each other accountable?

6. What could you do to build your network? What groups could you join?

"Believe in yourself, figure out what you really want your contribution to be, and go for it. Think strategically: how do you actually get there? Make the best use of your fantastic talents – and don't be shy about letting people know."

– Sally Helgesen

IT'S NOT ALL ABOUT YOU!

Leadership is about people

4

"As we look ahead into the next century, leaders will be those who empower others."

– Bill Gates

You're in the lunchroom at work getting a drink, and you can see a guy walking in your direction. Let's call him Nigel. You know he's coming your way. Your heart sinks. You turn away, trying to look busy. But it's no use.

You joined the company at the same time as Nigel did several years ago and you worked alongside each other. You used to be great friends, going out for lunch together, comparing experiences, sharing your aspirations for the future. But when Nigel was promoted to assistant manager of the department, everything changed.

So now Nigel walks into the lunchroom to get his coffee, and he starts bragging about his latest project and its success. He goes on and on as if he were the only person involved, yet you know many others worked with him. You try to get a word in, asking about those colleagues, but he cuts you off every time. All he wants to talk about is himself.

Eventually, he walks away with his arrogant swagger, taking his coffee with him, never bothering to ask how you are.

Do you know a Nigel?

***

From Far East to Middle East

After two great years in Singapore, it was time for me to move on. Someone I knew in Singapore had become principal of a business college in Bahrain in the Arabian Gulf. He asked me to join his team as head of the secretarial department. What an amazing opportunity! I quickly said yes. He didn't tell me much about the role, just that I'd be working with a Scottish girl named Patricia.

Before long, I found myself headed to another unknown. I'd never been to the Middle East and had no experience with the culture. As it was 1986 and there was no Google, I went to the library and found out as much as I could.

***

After a night in a hotel when I arrived, I learned I'd be sharing an apartment with Patricia, so I was keen to meet her. Unfortunately, she wasn't so warm towards me, and I soon discovered why. Patricia had worked at the college for six months before the new principal came in and started making changes. She wasn't happy that he was bringing in a new girl as head of department, instead of appointing her.

So, there I was, a new girl in a new job in a new country. At age 30, I found myself in a leadership situation with a colleague who was clearly not happy to meet me, and one other part-time teacher I'd yet to meet.

I was given a fabulous office on my own overlooking the Arabian Gulf. Patricia had a desk in the staffroom down the corridor together with the teachers from other departments. It didn't take long for me to realise this would just not work. Whenever Patricia and I talked, I could feel the tension around us. When I walked in the staffroom, all conversations stopped. And as I sat alone at my desk staring out at the beautiful view, I could almost feel the daggers in my back.

I phoned home often to keep in touch with Mum and Dad, who were eager to hear about my new job and new friends. My down-to-earth Dad came from a humble background. Friendly and good-humoured, he sang a lot and told jokes and limericks. He loved to make people laugh. You read earlier that my Dad worked in the Parks Department in Sheffield. Being jovial and good-natured, he soon made friends with all the visitors to the parks where he worked.

My Dad was a hard-working man, always doing the best job he could. He had no aspirations to climb the ladder or be a boss himself. But his co-workers did. Dad often came home from work telling stories about how they would suck up to their bosses. Then when one of them gained a promotion, he became the big "I am"! As Dad said this, he would hold his hands out from either side of his head, implying they had big heads, full of ego. Dad had no time for people like that. And he was just the opposite.

After listening to me explain my situation with Patricia, Dad said, "Just because Shirley's left Sheffield, it doesn't mean she should forget her roots. Don't become the big 'I am'!"

Don't become the big "I am".

I couldn't help but smile. I knew exactly what he meant, and I knew exactly what to do.

* * *

Back at work after the weekend, Patricia and I rearranged the furniture to add another desk, and my office soon became our office. From that day, everything started to change. Patricia and I were the only two full-time members of our department, so we had to strategise. Although I had no formal leadership training, I knew instinctively this could only work if Patricia and I worked together as a team. We interviewed together to find new part-time teachers for the department. We created timetables and designed the department's curriculum together. I may have had the title, but we shared the workload and the decisions. I was also careful to share the credit. In my monthly reports and presentations, I acknowledged Patricia's contributions and made it widely known that everything was a team effort.

This worked like a charm. I didn't just gain a great colleague; I gained a best friend.

Shirley and Patricia in Bahrain

"It takes just about the same amount of time to be a nice guy as it does to be a jerk."

– Mark Sanborn

My Dad

My Dad holding his home-grown carrots.

LESSON:

Don't be the big "I am"!

What if...?

What if I'd been the big "I am"?

What if I'd gotten too big for my boots?

What if I'd kept my office all to myself?

What if I'd taken the credit for everything?

In the two years I lived in Bahrain, Patricia and I helped build the secretarial department, with new part-time teachers, a full curriculum, and happy students. Soon after I left, Patricia was appointed deputy principal.

However, in my second year in Bahrain, my world came crashing down when the phone rang in the middle of the night. My Dad was in hospital after a massive heart attack. I told my Mum I would be home as quickly as I could. Patricia immediately took charge and arranged for my flight ticket and car hire. The following day, I was on my way home, praying my Dad would hold on until I arrived.

Mum and I went to the hospital every day to visit Dad. The doctors warned us he was unlikely to recover from this. I'll never forget when my friend Caroline came to the hospital with us. Dad had always made a big fuss of my friends, and Caroline was his favourite. As sick as he was in his hospital bed, my Dad smiled when he saw Caroline. He signalled us both to come closer because he had barely enough breath to speak.

That day, Dad told us a limerick he'd never told us before. He wanted to make us smile, and he certainly did that. Caroline and I felt guilty for making so much noise with our laughter in a ward full of cardiac patients.

Two days later, my Dad passed away. But he's in my heart, and I hope to always live by the principles he taught me.

> "Kindness trumps everything.
> Kind people are magnets for
> all of the good things in life."
>
> – Tom Giaquinto, *Be A Good Human*

Reflections from Fredrik Haren

Fredrik grew up in his native Sweden with an identical twin brother, Teo. He told me that when you grow up with someone else who looks like you, it's hard for one to feel more special than the other. Fredrik and Teo have always been close. They even chose the same vocation: professional speaking.

Fredrik Haren, global keynote speaker on creativity, change, and global mindset

Today, Fredrik travels the world as a professional speaker. He has lived in Singapore and been a member of Asia Professional Speakers Singapore (APSS) for several years. APSS is a not-for-profit association of professional and emerging speakers and trainers.

Every year, the APSS president chooses a theme for the year. When Fredrik became president in July 2018, he chose the theme "Better Together". This came from Sweden being known as a society of consensus. We know "consensus" means general agreement, yet the origins of the word tell us so much more.

"Con" means together, and "sensus" comes from the word *sentire*, meaning to feel. So the word "consensus" actually means to feel together.

For Fredrik, "Better Together" showed that he didn't want his presidential year to be all about him but rather about the association's members – that is, making everyone feel better by being in this group.

During his year at the helm, Fredrik made a commitment to meet as many APSS members and potential members as possible. He notched up a total of 160 one-to-one meetings, each one lasting at least an hour. That's 160 hours, about one month's full-time work! (The presidency is a pro-bono position that a professional speaker takes on as well as his/her regular speaking job.) He listened to members, found out more about them, mentored them, and made them feel an important part of the APSS community.

"Better Together" became a big hit with APSS members, and the association grew in spirit and strength as a result. At the association's annual convention, the theme inspired a balanced speaker roster of half male and half female, and with equal numbers of locals, foreigners, and mixed races.

Can we all learn something from Fredrik and the Swedish culture of consensus? I think we can.

Swedish leadership style has come to be characterised by easy communications, low internal competition, non-hierarchical organisational structures, and informal decision-making. Group consensus is the norm to ensure all individuals have a say, regardless of their status. In a Swedish company, for example, a new staff member might freely stop a managing director in the corridor to share an idea.

This style has spread to other countries, too. The HR manager of Volkswagen in Germany has coffee with everyone who starts work with the company on the person's first or second day. The president also makes it a point to meet every new employee. This company provides a great example of how to make everyone in the company feel heard.

Clearly, something about this "consensus" leadership style builds thriving teams. As far back as the 18th century, Sweden was the largest producer of iron ore in the world. In the 20th century, it became one of the pioneering countries in the Internet revolution.

Even Fredrik jumped on this bandwagon by starting an Internet company that grew to 60 employees in five years by hiring one new person every month.

Sweden has also produced some of the world's most recognisable brands, such as IKEA, Ericsson, H&M, Electrolux, and Volvo, not to mention such fast-growing start-ups as Spotify, Skype, and Mojang.

As the world gets smaller and the pace of innovation increases, anyone starting a business today might look into the Swedish "consensus" leadership style. This strong formula seems to bring out the best in people and create very successful teams.

 Reflections from Connecting the Dots. Watch exclusive interviews with all Shirley's guests.

"Leadership is about getting everyone to feel that they are better together."

– Fredrik Haren

Being a leader is not about you.
It's about people.

The more successful we are, the higher we climb, the more confidence and power we gain. What else comes with success? An inflated ego. Having a higher salary, a nicer office, and more benefits than others are all fine. Owning material things can make you feel like you've "arrived". But the truth is, you haven't.

Being a leader is not about you. It's about people.

You're probably thinking of people who fit in this category. They get an ounce of success and start lording it over everyone else. They become more selfish and disrespectful of others. They love the sound of their own voices and are likely to interrupt people. And if they ever receive criticism, they become defensive, so they don't learn from their mistakes.

Those who have inflated egos see and hear only what they want to. As a result, it's easy to lose touch with the people they lead as well as their customers and stakeholders.

As you climb the ladder, it's essential to keep your ego in check.

As you climb the ladder and achieve more success, it's critical to keep your ego in check. This is not always easy. It requires a lot of reflection, honesty, and courage. Together with humility and gratitude, these qualities form the core of being a great self-leader.

At the end of each day or week, take time to reflect on all the people who helped you. By doing that, you develop a sense of humility by recognising you were not the only one involved in your success. Don't hesitate to send a note of gratitude to those on your list.

10 ways to bring out the best in others

When you bring out the best in others, it creates a win-win in every direction. It gives you more time for the important work you have to do, and it increases the effectiveness of your team and the organisation overall.

Apart from anything else, though, bringing out the best in others is the right thing to do. Here are 10 ways you can do this:

1. **Get to know your team.**
   The best way to start is by finding out more about your team members. What are their current roles, how effective are they, what are their strengths and aspirations? Your team members will want you to succeed, because then the whole team will succeed. So, get to know them, help develop them, and allocate responsibilities thoughtfully. Then you're setting everyone up for success.

2. **Lead by example.**
   In my teacher training, I remember being told we had to "know the way, go the way, and show the way". The same goes for leaders. In the pages of this book, you'll read how certain people have inspired me. They include Linda Foster, my teacher in 1981, and Pam Forrester, who gave me the job in Singapore and became a mentor for life. You'll meet more as we journey through the chapters of this book. So, as a leader, or a potential leader, model the attitude, principles, and work ethics that you would like to see in others.

3. **Encourage them to speak up.**
   The last thing you need are what my Dad would call "Yes men" – people who keep their heads down, do their jobs, and barely share their thoughts or opinions, and just become followers. Encourage team members to speak up in meetings. This will give them confidence to speak up more. And it's also good for your ego as you learn to listen to others.

4. Empower them.

Most leaders are good at delegating tasks, but delegating is not the same as empowering. Empowering means sharing your power and your responsibility – just as I did in Bahrain with Patricia. We shared the responsibility to make decisions and solve problems. We faced challenges together. Indeed, it would never have worked any other way. As a result, our relationship became stronger, we both became more productive, and our department became more successful. Win-win-win!

> Leadership is not about being the best. It's about making everyone else better.

5. Encourage them.

It's a leader's job to help his or her people believe they can succeed. How? Show your team members you believe in them. Encourage them at every opportunity. Imagine how great they will feel to receive reinforcement from you. This will result in them becoming more committed to doing what they do. Then consider how they will feel if you don't give them encouragement. See the difference?

6. Give credit.

I was careful to give Patricia credit and praise in meetings and in my monthly reports to the principal. Giving public praise and recognition makes you look good and them feel great. You'll find it also increases their confidence and makes them more likely to want to do more.

7. **Coach them.**

As a leader, it's your job to give your team members honest feedback. Of course, they will make mistakes along the way. Slip-ups and oversights happen. It's your job to coach them through such events, but don't deliver feedback in ways that feel like criticism. Instead, be kind and constructive, and communicate with empathy. While giving practical advice, coach them about the way forward.

8. **Focus on serving, not self-serving.**

Some leaders focus on what's in it for them; the best leaders focus on serving others. Work to make your team, your department, and your organisation more successful.

9. **Ask for advice.**

No one gets to the top on their own. Successful people don't hesitate to ask for advice. Having someone you can look up to for coaching or mentoring is essential to becoming successful.

Successful people don't hesitate to ask for advice.

10. **Be a great follower, too.**

As a leader, you don't have to know it all. You can't know it all. Nor can you always be in charge. When you become a good follower, you become a good leader, too.

Your reflections

1. Think of two leaders you admire and respect. What characteristics do they share?

2. Think of a leader you do not admire and respect. Why?

3. Who has been a role model for you? What are their greatest qualities?

4. Who do you go to for advice or guidance?

5. Who comes to you for advice or guidance?

6. In what ways could you help your colleagues or team members to be more successful?

"It is literally true that you can succeed best and quickest by helping others to succeed."

– Napoleon Hill

IF YOU DON'T DO IT, SOMEONE ELSE WILL

One opportunity could change your life

5

"If we wait until we're ready, we'll be waiting for the rest of our lives. Let's go."

— Lemony Snicket, nom de plume of Daniel Handler, from *The Ersatz Elevator*

Think about someone you know. We'll call her Janet.

Like many of us, Janet leads a routine life. She gets up at the same time most days, has a set morning routine, follows the same route to work. When she walks into the office, she goes straight to her desk and starts going through all the tasks on her to-do list. Janet doesn't really think about her habitual tasks; she just goes through the motions of ticking things off her list. No wonder she often feels "stuck" in her role, wondering why others have moved on or up. But Janet stays right where she is and doesn't do anything about it.

At the same time, Janet sometimes allows herself to dream about starting a new job, finding a relationship, even losing weight. But she's too busy following her familiar routine to think about how to achieve any of these things. She also knows that change requires work, and that sounds too difficult.

Do you know a Janet, or maybe a John, who behaves this way? For them, probably the biggest obstacle to achieving their goals is fear. Fear of failure, fear of success, fear of the unknown, fear of looking foolish, fear of making the wrong decision, fear of embarrassment. With all these fears looming over Janet's head, no wonder she stays put in her familiar habits and routines.

Don't be like Janet (or John)!

* * *

A new passion begins

In 1989, I moved from Bahrain back to Singapore to work for the same school I did previously. One morning, the principal told me two representatives from a publishing company were in the reception area. She added, "They want to buy me lunch. Come with me." Never one to refuse a free lunch with two handsome guys, I went along to what would become a fateful meeting with Peter Marshall and David Buckland from the company that is now Pearson Education, one of the world's largest publishing companies.

Over lunch, the visitors wanted to know which books we asked the students to buy as class textbooks for their various subjects. I told them all the books they needed for Business Studies, Office Administration, Shorthand, and Typewriting. However, when it came to the subject of Business English, I had to say we didn't ask students to buy a book because I didn't feel one book was suitable. Ever since I'd started teaching Business English in 1983, I'd been looking for a great textbook but had never found one suitable. So, over the years, I had put together a course manual for students to use as a textbook, and it worked very well.

Peter Marshall's next words stunned me. "Will you write a book for us?" It turned out this was one of the reasons for their visit to our school that day.

I'd never dreamed of writing a book. But they persisted. They described a big gap in the market, and their company wanted to fill it. By the end of our lunch, I had promised to consider this opportunity and get back to them with my answer.

If you don't do it, someone else will.

I called my Mum that evening and told her my news. As I expected, Mum said, "Shirley, go for it. You can do this!" Then I called Pam Forrester at her home in the UK, and she said exactly the same thing. In fact, she uttered what became immortal words to me:

"If you don't do it, someone else will."

In the week that followed, I asked my boss if I could take three months unpaid leave to go back to Sheffield, do research, and write this book. Before long, I was back in Sheffield, where I worked solidly for three months. I included sections on how to write business letters, memos, reports, proposals, minutes. Lots of theory, lots of examples. And remember, there was no Google in those days. All my research came from bookstores and libraries.

I knew my good friend and mentor Pam would always be at the other end of the telephone for guidance. She also sent me lots of past Business English examination papers from the LCCI Examinations Board. These were the examinations that students using the book would aim to pass, so I put a lot of exam questions in the book, plus sample answers I created myself.

I thoroughly enjoyed focusing solely on this huge project. And it was fun taking the train to London on various trips to meet the publishers at their offices. After three months of writing about writing, I proudly presented my completed draft to the publisher for production.

My first book, *Communication for Business*, was published in 1992 by Pearson Education. It became the main textbook used by many colleges worldwide for students aiming to pass Business English examinations of the LCCI Examinations Board. By 2002, I had revised it four times.

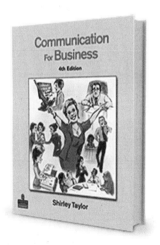

While that in itself was amazing to me, I could never have imagined how many other book opportunities would come as a result of this.

***

The year after *Communication for Business* was published, the same publishers in London called. "Shirley, do you know the book *Model Business Letters* by Leonard Gartside?" In my studies with Linda Foster, she often referred us to information in his book, and I always kept a copy on my bookshelf. Teaching in Singapore, I often referred to his latest edition. The lady on the phone then said, "Well, bad news, Shirley. Unfortunately, Mr. Gartside has died. But good news! We want you to revise his book."

What an opportunity. But my old demons came back to haunt me. Was I good enough to do this? Would I fail? Again, I talked to my Mum, even though I knew what she would say. Again, I asked Pam for advice, even though I knew what she would say...

"If you don't do it, someone else will!"

Filling this author's shoes seemed like an enormous task. His first three editions of this book had sold thousands of copies all over the world and been translated into several languages. But of course, I accepted the challenge, and I worked hard researching and writing the fourth edition of *Model Business Letters*. It was published in 1992, this time not only with the original author's name but with mine too.

Over the years, I've updated this book many times because, as with most things, writing changes. The title of this book has also evolved, with the seventh edition being *Model Business Letters, Emails and Other Business Documents* (2012).

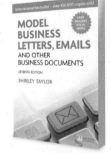

As a result of these first two books, there has been a domino effect. I've also received opportunities from other publishers to write many other books. One series that I spearheaded resulted in a total of nine books. There have also been opportunities where I collaborated with other authors to write books together.

During this second visit to Singapore, I recruited another expat teacher from the north of England, Lesley. It was great having an ally, and we had good fun too exploring local bars and nightclubs, and meeting new friends.

One wonderful thing about living in Singapore was its proximity to some wonderful islands in Malaysia. When we discovered Rawa, we travelled there with friends regularly for long weekends away. What fun we had staying in chalets on the beach, snorkelling and swimming in the South China Sea, and kayaking around the island.

After a couple of years, Lesley and I went back to England again. We both were offered jobs at the same college in Kuwait. It was another "do I, don't I?" decision to make. But this time, while Lesley said 'yes', I said 'no', choosing to stay in the UK. This didn't stop us keeping in touch over the years, even though many years went by without seeing each other.

Lesley and her family now live back in England, so we were able to meet up again in Brighton in 2019. What an amazing reunion it was. We are looking forward to seeing much more of each other when I move back to the UK soon. Lesley is definitely another 'dot' in my journey of life.

Shirley and Lesley, snorkelling in Rawa in 1992, and reuniting in Brighton in 2019

Peter Marshall

Peter Marshall, now Managing Director, ELT, at Oxford University Press

LESSON:

If you don't do it, someone else will!

What if...?

What if I hadn't accepted my boss's invitation to join the publishers for lunch?

What if Peter and David hadn't encouraged me?

What if I'd said "no" immediately because of having no dreams to write a book?

What if Mum, Dad, and Pam had not encouraged me?

What if I couldn't find the courage to say "yes"?

Seriously, I often wonder, "How the heck did Shirley from Sheffield end up as a published author and a leading expert in business writing and email writing skills?"

I often think of my old headmaster at school telling my parents I would never come to anything. What would he think of all that's happened?

"A pessimist sees the difficulty in every opportunity; an optimist sees the opportunity in every difficulty."

– Sir Winston Churchill

Reflections from Julie Holmes

Julie often describes the leadership journey not as a ladder that we climb but a jungle gym. We move upwards, sometimes we take a step back, sometimes sideways. But we're always moving in different directions and making choices about where to go next.

Julie Holmes, speaker, inventor, entrepreneur, innovation expert (www.julieholmes.com)

This has certainly proved to be the case for Julie. After earning her master's degree in communication, she taught communication, influence, and organisational communication for several years. However, while she loved teaching, she didn't see it taking her where she wanted to go, even though she didn't quite know where that was!

Living in Omaha, Nebraska, around 1997, Julie started going through the many steps required to apply to join the candidate school of the Air Force. She was well under way with her application, when, on a whim one day, she went along to a career fair. At this event, organisations, recruiters and schools gave information to potential employees. Julie printed out lots of résumés on beautiful paper and handed them out to everyone she met there.

She soon received a call from a technology company, saying, "We think your background and skills would be an exceptional fit for how we communicate about our products to our customers and our users. Would you be interested in working with us?"

So now Julie was torn as she faced two open doors in front of her. One door would take her into the military and a predictable career with lots of rules to follow. The other door would take her into the unknown, where she might be able to make her own rules. Julie had to think hard to decide which door to walk through.

Never being good at following rules, Julie chose to forget the military and accept the corporate job. Given a choice of seven cities in the US where the company had offices, Julie chose Denver, Colorado. There, she not only faced getting used to a new job but a new city, too.

Accepting this opportunity started a brand-new career that spanned decades. Julie loved her job and worked with some of the world's biggest organisations. She learned a lot about how quickly it's possible to create products and get them on sale, and also about serving customers in many different ways.

And all this happened because she grabbed a new opportunity and took a chance on something different.

Julie loved to travel, so she enjoyed visiting clients all over the US and Europe. Going to Dublin, Ireland, for the first time was especially exciting for her. Little did she know what fate had in store, because that's where she met her future husband.

> When we start opening ourselves up to possibilities, the universe conspires to help us.

Two decades later, after living in the UK for many years, Julie has come full circle. With her husband, their two children, and their dog, she now lives in Denver again. But, instead of coming up with new products and ideas for a corporation, Julie now has her own business inventing products that are sent to dozens of countries worldwide. She also speaks to audiences all over the world on how to think like an inventor and grab opportunities whenever possible.

Reflections from Connecting the Dots.
Watch exclusive interviews with all
Shirley's guests.

> "A true leader sees possibilities – in people, products, strategy and more – and then creates plans to make it reality. What possibilities do you see?"
>
> – Julie Holmes

Opportunity and you

Do you know people who complain about their situation, their job, or their lifestyle but don't do anything about changing it? It's quite ironic, isn't it?

Are there any opportunities that are staring you in the face?

It could be they don't have a great longing for change. Perhaps it's because change carries huge risks and it's scary. Yet, even when we're unhappy with our current situation, it's still familiar. Change is so uncertain. Because of this, many people miss opportunities, and some don't even see them when staring them in the face. We've already looked at many opportunities that came along for me – times when I could have said "no" but instead I said "yes".

However, let me bare my soul and share the other side of the coin. I can also remember times (yes, more than one!) when I'd been in a relationship for a few years, and I kept feeling it wasn't what I wanted. But the relationship felt "comfortable" and a voice in my head would say, "Maybe it'll work out" or "Do you want to start again on your own?" When my partner was the one who pulled the plug on the relationship, of course it upset me. But it wasn't long before that changed to complete relief.

How many people stay in a familiar relationship or a comfortable job because of fear of the unknown?

Just like in the story about Janet (or John), fear often gets in the way of achieving goals. People stay in familiar habits, routines, and relationships because of fear. Fear of failure, success, embarrassment. Fear of the unknown. Fear of looking foolish. And if they lack confidence – no matter how unhappy they are – it's easier to stay safe in the familiar.

I have to admit I have my familiar favourites. When visitors come to Singapore (where I live as I write this book), I take them to my favourite restaurant. It's where I know the food and ambience will be great. If I choose a new-to-me restaurant, I might not enjoy it and I'd feel embarrassed to have taken my visitors there.

However, when someone invited me to lunch recently, I admit to feeling nervous at being in an unknown part of town and eating at a strange restaurant. Guess what? It ended up being a great experience, and I have been back many times. Thanks, Cathy!

Count the risks

As you go through your day today, count the number of risks you take – every time you cross the road, take a train, make a presentation, or go to a networking event full of strangers. Although these are minor risks compared with starting a new job or moving to a new country, they are risks you take regularly.

> The stimuli for feeling nervous are exactly the same as the stimuli for excitement!

> "In a world that's changing really quickly, the only strategy that is guaranteed to fail is not taking risks."
>
> – Mark Zuckerberg

I love Simon Sinek's presentations, especially the one in which he says, "We need to change the narrative." He gave examples of how, at the Olympics, media interviewers asked each elite athlete, "Were you nervous?" Every single athlete replied, "No, I was excited." Think about it. The stimuli for feeling nervous often include a racing heart, sweaty palms, and visualising an unknown future. What are the stimuli for excitement? A racing heart, sweaty palms, and visualising an unknown future.

This story has helped me change my narrative, and this can change my state of mind and ultimately change the outcomes I experience.

8 ways to change your narrative

Are you ready to start changing your narrative and be open to opportunities? Do you want to create new scenarios and replace nerves and fear with excitement and curiosity? Here are eight suggestions for you. Try them and see what doors of opportunity open for you.

1. **Make a list.**
   Write down all the risks you've already taken that have been positive experiences. Perhaps it was learning to drive, going to college, taking a holiday on your own, moving to a new city, joining a dance class. What would you have missed if you hadn't taken these opportunities?

2. **Start small.**

   Act on small opportunities whenever you can. Smile at a stranger in the grocery store queue and start a conversation. Try a different kind of food or café. Wear something in a different colour. Then notice what happens. Before you do something new, ask yourself, "What's the worst that could happen, and what's the best thing that could happen?" Decide which one outweighs the other. "Is it worth the risk?"

3. **Be proactive.**

   It can be frustrating hearing about a colleague being awarded a new project to work on, or perhaps moving to a position you would have liked. Instead of feeling upset, ask yourself, "What could I have done better to position myself for this opportunity?" Your superiors aren't mind readers, so discuss your aspirations for career development with them.

4. **Be aware of your impact.**

   The smile you give, the way you answer your phone, your voice on your voicemail, how you greet strangers – everything you do creates an impact. It might be a good impact, or it might not. Make it a habit to consider how every action you take will affect the people around you. Ask yourself, "Am I making it easy and pleasant for people to work with me, or am I making it difficult?"

5. **Say "yes" more often.**

   When I first came to Singapore, I remember a colleague asking me many times if I'd like to go out deep-sea fishing with her husband and friends. I said "no, thank you" so many times, they stopped asking. It took a couple of years before I got the nerve to ask if I could go with them. When I did go, I had an amazing weekend! Don't live with regrets. Say "yes". Thanks, Sally and Henry.

6. **Make new friends.**

   In my work, I meet many people with jobs in large office blocks. Their organisation is often on several floors. If this sounds like your organisation, don't keep "you" to yourself. Get out of your silo and connect with other people. This could happen in the lunchroom, in the lift, at a local café, or walking along the street. Start a conversation with someone you've never spoken to but who works in your company. Such a connection could start a great friendship. It could also mean that person thinks of you when an opportunity comes up in his or her department.

7. **Put up your hand.**
   Look for opportunities to serve on a project team or a committee at work or socially. Serving can feel rewarding and bring many benefits your way. (You'll read examples of this in later chapters of this book.)

8. **Make time to think.**
   In our busy lives, it's often not easy to focus. Find some time to sit down quietly on your own and just think. Take time away from the day-to-day hustle of life to contemplate what's happening, where you want to be, and what you want to do. My good friend Nishant (you met him in Chapter 2) has an annual ritual of going on his own to sit near the Singapore Merlion. The Merlion is the official mascot of Singapore, a mythical creature with a lion's head and the body of a fish. Nishant leaves his phone at home so he has no distractions, and he stays the whole day. He takes a notepad and writes down whatever comes to him. This ritual normally sets his course for the following year.

> **"The ladder of success is best climbed by stepping on the rungs of opportunity."**
>
> – Ayn Rand

Your reflections

1. Make a list of all the risks you've already taken that have resulted in positive experiences.

2. Look back at the reflections section of Chapter 3 to think again about opportunities where you wished you'd said "yes" instead of "no".

3. What is one small opportunity or risk you could take today?

4. What's the *worst* thing that could happen with this?

What's the *best* thing that could happen?

5. At your workplace, what project or committee could you ask to take part in?

6. Where could you spend the morning, the afternoon or the whole day, by yourself with no distractions, just thinking and writing? Will you?

"When someone offers you an amazing opportunity, and you're not sure if you can do it... say yes, and figure it out later!"

– Sir Richard Branson

YOU CAN BE A LEADER, WHATEVER YOUR TITLE

Leadership with a small "l"

6

"Become the kind of leader that people would follow voluntarily; even if you had no title or position."

– Brian Tracy

Your company has introduced special service awards this year for the first time. Your boss, a divisional head, has been appointed as chair of a special committee to arrange the awards evening. He needs one person from his department to help him organise the event. He's wondering who's the best person to choose. He's considering two people, Winnie and Rekha, who both joined the company two years before.

Winnie is quite reserved and shy. She knows her job well, works hard, and is highly task-oriented. When taking on extra work, she does what she's asked to do efficiently. She's reliable and hardworking. When attending meetings, she's usually quiet and does not contribute unless directly asked. Winnie has a few close company friends to lunch with, and you rarely see her chit-chatting at work. At appraisal time, she says she's happy with her work but has no interest in climbing the ladder. She takes feedback well, and she attends training programmes when her boss suggests them.

Rekha is cheerful and friendly, thorough and reliable. A detail person, she makes daily checklists and happily takes on extra tasks when asked. She takes an interest in learning more about the division's work and often helps others. Rekha has made many friends and often lunches with colleagues from other divisions. In meetings, she regularly contributes ideas and makes useful comments. At appraisal time, she takes feedback well and is quick to select training courses she'd like to attend to develop her skills.

Do you think the boss should choose Winnie or Rekha? Why?

***

Back to Blighty

In the early 1990s, I lived back home in Sheffield again. Since my Dad had passed away in 1989, I knew my Mum wasn't getting any younger, so I wanted to spend more time with her. I soon found a part-time teaching post at a local Further Education college, but I didn't really enjoy it. Working in Singapore and Bahrain, I'd had a taste of more responsibility and different projects that had stretched my abilities. Teaching shorthand and typewriting in Sheffield didn't make me feel fulfilled or keep me busy.

At that time, Pam Forrester was still chief examiner for some of the examinations on the LCCIEB Private and Executive Secretary's Diploma course. She asked me to join her team of assistant examiners for the subject Manuscript Transcription. I didn't take any persuading, and I loved this new role.

Every few months, I went to London with about eight other assistant examiners for a meeting led by Pam. We discussed the examination papers and finalised the marking scheme we all had to follow. After those meetings, I went home and settled down into the routine of marking exam papers. Each assistant examiner had to first mark ten exam papers and send them to Pam to make sure everyone's marking met the same standard. As soon as Pam gave her approval, it was all systems go. I sat at my desk for hours marking hundreds of students' examination papers from all over the world.

I learned a lot from Pam during this time, and I took to heart all the advice and guidance she gave to me. And I always made it a point to do a great job; I didn't ever want to let her down.

A year or two after that, Pam retired from her position as chief examiner and she was asked to recommend someone to take over this role. I was so honoured when she asked me, and I was thrilled to accept. So now it was *my* job to create the examination papers and lead a team of my own assistant examiners. Pam's were big shoes to fill, but I had her guidance every step of the way.

***

Looking back, I think my leadership skills were being developed for as long as I'd known Pam. When I started teaching in Singapore in 1983, Pam had mentored me as I took on more responsibilities. As one of many Business English teachers, I led a project to put together a master file

You may be developing leadership skills over many years without realising it.

of resources. This involved working with the other Business English teachers to design student handouts, answer sheets, visual teaching aids, and transparencies. This way, instead of the teachers doing their own thing, we shared our resources and combined our ideas.

When I moved to Bahrain, Pam guided me in my new role as head of department, holding working sessions with me and Patricia to discuss best practices.

Back in the UK, I could see Pam had been grooming me to take over her position as chief examiner. I took to the job like a duck to water, especially the creative aspect of this role. My ideas started to flow, keeping me up late into the evening crafting the examination papers and the model answers to go with them. The eagle eye who would check through them and suggest amendments was, of course, Pam. I always valued her input and suggestions for improvement.

The next thing I knew, the LCCI examinations board asked me to write a book in its "How to Pass..." series. Yet another challenge – and again I enjoyed the creativity required. *How to Pass Manuscript Transcription* was published in 1995. For years, teachers all over the world used it to guide their students to pass this important and relatively new examination.

With so many changes in the transcription examination criteria at that time, I'd heard rumours that there would be a big meeting to go through the changes and marking criteria in detail. But I never imagined I would receive a phone call from the division head asking if I would lead this meeting at its London head office. With more than 30 examiners being invited, I was expected to present all the changes to the examinations in detail, and the reasoning behind them, as well as talk everyone through the new marking schemes.

Have you ever struggled with the imposter syndrome?

What an incredible opportunity for me. I admit I didn't accept the job without some fear and trepidation. You can't imagine how many times I thought, "Gosh! What's happening? I'm just Shirley from Sheffield!" Coincidentally, that's when I first heard the term "imposter syndrome" – something I felt many times before and since. It's when deep down you feel like a fraud; you feel unworthy; you believe your accomplishments result from chance. We'll look at this syndrome more in Chapter 7.

I threw myself into the project, preparing thoroughly for this important training programme. I wanted the "powers that be" to know they had been right to put their trust in me. People from all over the UK would attend, many of them older and more experienced than me. And guess who else would be there? Yes, not only Pam Forrester but also my Mum, who was an assistant examiner in the same subjects.

The meeting took place in the mid-1990s when the Internet, laptops and projectors weren't commonplace. So, for my presentation, I had to use an overhead projector and transparencies. (If this is before your time, Google them.) I burnt lots of midnight oil preparing for this programme.

Finally, the big day arrived. I hardly slept the night before I had to travel to London on the train with Mum. Preceding my main presentation would be a welcome lunch with speeches by the CEO of the examinations board as well as the division head. I was almost sick with nerves. At this time, I hadn't learned an important lesson that you just read about in the previous chapter: that the stimuli for nerves are identical to the stimuli for excitement. I could have told myself "I'm excited" instead of "I'm nervous", because it works like a charm!

I've always loved this quote from Confucius: "Success depends upon previous preparation, and without such preparation there is sure to be failure."

I'd had this quote up on my wall as I got ready for this important training, and the preparation certainly paid off! I'm pleased to say the day was a huge success.

"Success depends upon previous preparation, and without such preparation there is sure to be failure."

– Confucius

Pam Forrester (again)

My last visit with Pam, her sister and nephew.

LESSON:

Learning to lead can start from any position, at any time.

What if...?

What if I hadn't built a strong relationship with Pam Forrester since she interviewed me for my first teaching job in 1983?

What if I hadn't done the best job I could in Singapore and Bahrain, giving Pam confidence in me and my leadership skills?

What if I didn't do a great job as an assistant examiner under Pam's guidance?

What if I hadn't taken on any leadership roles?

What if I had struggled with the imposter syndrome and said "no"?

I enjoyed being chief examiner of the examinations board for several years while back in the UK. Together, Mum and I must have marked thousands of examination papers from every part of the globe!

During that time, Mum and I also joined Weight Watchers. After reaching my goal weight, I wanted to help others, so I trained to be a leader within the organisation. Before long, I was taking on nine Weight Watchers classes a week!

Yes, life was busy, juggling different projects at the same time. I felt energised each morning and couldn't wait to get started. Feeling motivated led to being more productive. My creativity skyrocketed, with lots of ideas coming to me all the time, both for my examinations work and my Weight Watchers meetings. It was a very happy, positive time in my life.

Reflections from Mark Sanborn

It was such an honour for me to interview the author of one of my favourite books, *The Fred Factor*. A professional speaker who has provided coaching and leadership training to leaders for over 30 years, Mark Sanborn shared that many leaders told him stories about employees who do great leadership work but don't have a title. Mark has always been fascinated by this concept.

Mark Sanborn, international leadership speaker and bestselling author

One day, he was talking to the vice president of a technology company who said he had an important project and needed to find a leader. He approached Bob, a man on his team, saying it was a project he would be able to do well. The VP told Bob, "Leading the project will take a lot of work, but it's essential to the success of the team." Before saying if he would accept the project, Bob asked if he would get a new title. He wanted a concrete benefit to go with his efforts.

Bob's attitude made the VP stop and consider his request carefully. He then retracted his offer and went back to the drawing board, looking for someone else. He thought of Gail, a freelancer, who had always done a good job and shown promise.

When he spoke to Gail about leading this project, the VP said, "By the way, if you take on this project, I can't give you a title or make you a leader in the organisation." Her perfect response was, "That's fine. I don't need a title to be a leader."

This "aha" moment for Mark became the genesis for one of his bestselling books, *You Don't Need a Title to Be a Leader.* In his book, Mark suggests that leaders are not born; rather, they *learn* to lead. That means, whatever your title, you may not be aware of how much of a leader you already are!

> **It's not the title or the job you *have* that makes a difference. It's the job you *do* that makes a difference.**

Mark believes a title may give you power *over* people, but leadership is power *with* people. So even if you don't have formal leadership authority, what's important is your ability to create results with others – to build relationships, to collaborate, to innovate.

His advice is, "Don't let your lack of a title hold you back. You *are* a leader." Of course, he refers to leadership with a small "l", and it doesn't matter what your title is – whether you're a clerk or an accountant, a manager or a salesperson, a secretary or a business owner. Being a leader is about all the small things you can do every day to positively influence your customers, your colleagues, your stakeholders, your friends, your communities.

Mark suggests that you, too, can aspire to lead if you want to:

- take control of your life
- make your organisation better
- seize new opportunities
- improve the service your customers receive
- influence others to be their best
- solve problems
- contribute to the betterment of others
- make the world a little better

And you don't need a title to do it!

Reflections from Connecting the Dots. Watch exclusive interviews with all Shirley's guests.

"Leaders are people who make a positive difference, who make an impact on others and in the organisation through what they do and how they do it."

– Mark Sanborn

Leadership with a small "I" and you

In my work as a speaker and trainer, I love sharing how every one of us can make a difference. But it's amazing how, when asked, many audience members don't believe they have the ability and skills to make a real difference in the workplace.

> Everyone makes a difference. Some make a small difference; others make a big difference. What difference will *you* make?

In contrast, I tell them that every single person *does* make a difference. In some cases, it could be a small difference; in others, it could be a big difference (and sadly in a few it will be a negative difference, but let's not focus on that).

In our constantly changing, high-tech world, we feel pressed for time, pushed for results, and stressed to succeed. Because of this, people mostly focus on getting their immediate job done. However, I encourage them to focus on relationships, too. I call this "making a human difference". Amid the fast-paced action of our working day are numerous opportunities to affect someone's life – to make a human difference.

Think about it. With the rise of artificial intelligence, machines are taking over certain jobs. Yes, machines can take care of transactional aspects of work; they can get the job done. But as humans, we have

> Make a human difference every day!

one huge advantage over machines: inside our chests is a beating heart! We can all make a human difference in some way.

Here are a few simple things you can do every day to make a human difference:

- Nod, smile, and say "good morning" when you walk into the office.
- Say "hello" to people when you enter an elevator.
- Bring muffins to work on a Friday morning.
- Warm up your email messages with a human touch.
- Use the person's name several times in a phone conversation.
- Have lunch with someone you don't normally spend time with.
- Tell someone "great job!" and mean it.
- Say "thank you" often.
- Initiate a conversation with your taxi or Uber driver.
- Volunteer your time to a good cause.
- Raise funds for charity.
- Smile! It will make others smile, too.

This is just a short list to get you thinking. Why not commit to making a human difference with at least three people you come across every day? When you are managing three actions easily, up your game to include six people, and so on.

You have been given a life that no one else has. Its significance and direction are largely up to you. Whether you're young or not so young, it's never too late to start making a positive human difference to others. And when you do, people will notice. And you never know what opportunities might follow.

Lead yourself first

If leaders are not born but are people who learn to lead, then how can we fast-track our learning? We can do that by first becoming a great self-leader. Why is this important? Because at the heart of leadership is a person who makes a difference. And that could be you!

> At the heart of leadership is a person who makes a difference. And that could be you!

Potential leaders often become great by developing their self-leadership skills first. But this doesn't happen by accident. It requires daily practice, attention, and focus to make progress.

6 key traits of a great self-leader

1. **Believe you have something to offer.**
   Good self-leaders realise they have something to offer the world, not necessarily to change the world. Whether you are a clerk in the finance department or an admin executive in marketing, know you have something valuable to offer, something that is needed. Believe that you can have a positive influence on your colleagues, your department, and your organisation every day.

2. **Develop self-awareness.**
   Self-awareness means monitoring your inner world, your thoughts, your emotions, and your behaviours as they happen. Experts tell us to work towards a non-judgemental reflection, but this is not always easy. If you have ever thought, "I wish I hadn't done or said that," then you know what I mean. Next time you judge something you did, ask yourself: "How can I learn from this? What can I do differently next time?" Being able to monitor our emotions, actions and behaviours as they happen is the key to understanding ourselves better. Self-aware people tend to act

consciously and have a more positive outlook on life. They are also more likely to show compassion to others.

3. **Be confident.**
   More than half of human communication comes from nonverbal cues. This is something you could start working on immediately. Stand tall, with good posture. Develop a firm handshake. Maintain soft but direct eye contact. Use appropriate facial expressions rather than a dead-pan face.

   Another way to develop more confidence is to slow down your speech. So many people speak too quickly, but once you slow down, it serves to increase your confidence. Vary your tone of voice as you talk. Catch yourself if you notice yourself playing with a pen or fidgeting in any way.

   > Confident people win people over because it inspires others to be confident, too.

4. **Interact with people.**
   You can't escape it. Wherever you are on the career ladder, it's unlikely you'll never have to work with people. So, start becoming better at it! Initiate interactions rather than waiting for them. Be sincere in your interactions with your colleagues and team mates. Listen to them. Be interested in them. Encourage them. Respect their work and their efforts. Talk to them and get to know them. Find out what motivates them. Offer help where you can.

5. **Take action.**

Self-leadership means taking an active approach to life, being an actor rather than a spectator. Doing a great job, getting results, building relationships, and interacting with others are all important. But it's your *actions* that build your reputation. Successful leaders and self-leaders have the courage to take action while others hesitate. Don't just notice that something needs doing; do it. Don't just discuss a problem; fix it. Don't passively sit on the bench watching life happen; take an active part in it – at your workplace, at home, and socially, too. Your actions could even inspire others to do the same.

6. **Take a self-audit.**

Have an honest conversation with yourself and assess your strengths and weaknesses. Ask some close friends for their input. The first step to self-improvement is to admit you may not be perfect. Self-mastery starts with self-honesty. So, push aside your pride and ego; own up to what needs fixing in you. It can be hugely liberating. Transforming your inner personal world will ripple into your outer world, too.

Work on being a leader with a small "I" every day. Focus on doing the best job you can. Use your initiative. Get better at what you do. Get involved in your team and your organisation. Put up your hand to get involved in projects. Work on making a positive difference – a human difference!

> **Work on being a leader with a small "I" every day.**

Your first step? Think of yourself as being a leader with a small "I", and then – who knows where it may lead?

Your reflections

1. Do you believe you can shape your life and your career? How?

2. Do you usually focus on getting your job done, or do you also focus on relationships?

3. What changes could you commit to making immediately?

4. What is one way you have made a difference to another person during the past week?

5. What are at least three ways you will commit to making a difference to someone within the coming week?

6. Make a three-column table on a sheet of notepaper and complete each column:

My strengths	My weaknesses	My goals

Be honest as you can. If necessary, ask your closest friends to help. In your "My goals" column, be sure to state how you will achieve those goals and set deadlines for each of them.

"Better is the most important step to becoming your best. If you want to be your best, you need to start by getting better Start doing better. Good, better, best. That's how it works."

– Mark Sanborn

IT'S TIME TO CHANGE THE SCRIPT. YOU ARE WORTHY!

The imposter syndrome
strikes again

7

*"I have written eleven books,
but each time I think,
'Uh oh, they're going to find
out now. I've run a game
on everybody, and they're
going to find me out."*

– Maya Angelou

Even some of the most successful people struggle with "imposter syndrome". Deep down, they feel like a fraud, feeling everything they achieve is the result of pure luck or coincidence.

Does this sound familiar? You feel like someone might find you out. You'll make a mistake and soon it will all come tumbling down. The voice in your head keeps ringing, "How have I got away with it this far?" or "Can I really do what I've promised?" or "Pretty soon they'll find out I'm a phony."

The imposter syndrome can strike anyone at any level at any time. Starting college or university can often bring it on, making you question your own abilities. Starting a new job may trigger those feelings, wondering if you are the right person for the role.

Self-talk can be cruel, so it's time to change the script. You are *worthy*. You are *smarter* than you think. You are *better* than you think. You *know more* than you give yourself credit for. You are here for a reason.

Remember this, and remind yourself often!

* * *

Me? I'm just Shirley from Sheffield

On one of my return visits to Singapore in 1995, I met with my publisher's representative, my good friend Leslie Lim. He had arranged for me to promote my book in what was then the largest bookstore in Asia, Borders. I had

The imposter syndrome strikes again!

to deliver a 15-minute talk in the middle of a bookstore. My first thought was, "Who the heck wants to listen to me?" When I arrived, I saw a small area with about 20 seats. The voice in the back of my head kept taunting me. "There will be no one in those seats." "Who are you kidding?" "Why should they listen to you?"

I heard the announcer on the loudspeaker say, "Shirley Taylor will be giving a talk at two o'clock on the importance of good writing skills." I felt sick and kept running to the bathroom. As the time got closer to two o'clock, not one person was sitting in the seats. By the top of the hour, I was panicking even more. I could see lots of people behind bookshelves reading, or pretending to read. They kept glancing my way and then looking straight back at the books.

Right at two o'clock, I took the microphone and said the first words I could think of: "Hi there, I'm Shirley Taylor. I'm the one over here in the red jacket feeling very silly right now because I'm talking to myself. I have a copy of my book here for the first person to come over here and shake my hand."

Bingo! Several people rushed over to shake my hand and say hello, one of them delighted to receive the book. I encouraged them to sit down to listen, and they did. The icing on the cake was when several people stayed behind to line up, buy my book, and have me sign it.

***

Also on that visit, Leslie arranged for me to visit some secretarial and business colleges in Singapore and meet their teachers and students. They had been using my first two Business English books and were excited to see me in person. I was treated like royalty with photographs, speeches, interviews, and gifts.

After many visits that day, Leslie said, "There's just one more person I'd like you to meet." I remember saying, "Oh gosh, Leslie, haven't we done enough already?" He told me he had a good feeling about visiting Mrs. Wong, although an appointment hadn't been set up yet. Still I grumbled, telling him I was exhausted, but Leslie was persuasive. I rubbed my sore feet, put on my lippie and my smile, and off we went.

Mrs. Wong told us about the business school she was opening soon in conjunction with Beijing Foreign Studies University. She planned to introduce LCCI examination courses there. I chatted politely and told her I'd be happy to help. When she said she would be in touch once everything was in place, I didn't hold out any hope. Shortly after that, Leslie dropped me off for a much-needed reflexology session, and I soon forgot all about our visit with Mrs. Wong.

✳ ✳ ✳

Back home in Sheffield a few months later, I was surprised to receive a fax message (yes, fax, it was 1995, remember!) from Mrs. Wong. She told me her newly appointed manager in Beijing, Iris Tan, would be in touch with me to arrange a visit. Iris then faxed and introduced herself as the manager of the Beijing business school. She asked if I would visit Beijing in November to provide training for teachers and guidance for students.

That voice echoed in my ear again. "You're just Shirley from Sheffield." "You don't have a degree." "Somehow you've managed to write a couple of books." "By some fluke, you're now chief examiner for the LCCI Examinations Board." "It'll all come tumbling down soon!"

I then turned around this self-talk and asked the question I've asked myself many times since: "What would Pam say?" Even though I knew the answer, I called her to discuss this opportunity. Once again, she gave me great advice and support as she uttered those immortal words: "If you don't do it, someone else will!"

***

Several months later, after lots of faxes back and forth and all arrangements made, I found myself on a plane to Beijing.

Have you ever met someone who, on first sight, you knew would be a friend forever? Well, that's what happened when I met Iris Tan. When she greeted me at the airport, we both felt as though we'd known each other for ages. She made me feel so welcome and was a wonderful host while in Beijing. Visiting China was a big culture shock for me. At the time, China had only been open to independent travellers for just over a decade, so tourism was still in its infancy. What an eye-opener it was! I was grateful to have Iris as my host and translator.

I spent a lot of time at the business school giving presentations to students as well as guidance to the teachers on teaching techniques. On one occasion after delivering a session for students, a teacher asked, "Shirley, I've been watching you with our students. How do you manage to get them so involved and engaged in your lessons?" She told me she found it difficult to get students to speak up in her classes.

After delving deeper into how she conducted her classes, it became obvious that she used a "telling" style, where she just told the students the information they needed to know. A lesson I'd learned at teacher training college came back to me: "Never tell them what they could tell you!" I explained this to the young teacher, encouraging her to ask careful questions and elicit key information from the students.

Then, when the students answered, she could praise them and encourage more answers.

It was like I'd handed her a piece of gold. She had just never thought of doing that. This teacher never stopped thanking me, and I was pleased to see transformation in her teaching during my visit.

By the end of my time in Beijing, Iris had introduced me to lots of different food and taken me around loads of tourist areas, including some fabulous hotels. She'd also given me a great opportunity to talk to her students, offer guidance to her teachers, and provide mentorship to her on how to help students pass LCCIEB examinations. I will always treasure the gift of a beautiful cloisonné plate she presented me with that is proudly displayed on my wall.

***

By the way, something else happened during the same visit to Singapore when I met Mrs. Wong. My friend Leslie Lim and I had this unforgettable conversation.

Leslie:	"Shirley, I've heard there's someone in Singapore teaching full-day training programmes on business writing, and she recommends your book to everyone."
Me:	"Wow! That's great to hear!"
Leslie:	"Well, I don't think it's great. *You* should be teaching those full-day workshops."
Me:	"Me? No, I've been a teacher for years, but I've never done anything like a full-day programme."

Leslie: "So why not start
              now? And then you'll
              be promoting your
              own book."

> If someone else can do it, so can you!

Me: (In my head) "Me?
              I'm just Shirley from Sheffield…"

But of course, Leslie had planted the seed in my head. I soon heard the narrative again telling me lots of negative things. But this time, I also heard Pam's voice saying, "If others can do it, so can you."

So, I changed my self-talk and got to work!

***

Are you wondering what happened to Iris? Well since that visit to Beijing in 1995, Iris and I became great friends. She moved back to Singapore and now runs her own business. Over the years, we have holidayed together many times, and we have become great mentors and friends. Iris is another 'dot' in my journey of life.

Shirley and Iris in China 1995

On a breezy day in New Zealand 2018

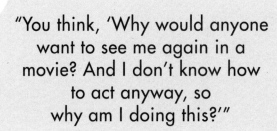

"You think, 'Why would anyone want to see me again in a movie? And I don't know how to act anyway, so why am I doing this?'"

– Meryl Streep

Leslie Lim

Shirley and Leslie Lim

LESSON:

It's time to change the narrative. You are worthy!

What if...?

What if I'd told Leslie "no" when he asked me to visit just one more person?

What if I hadn't met Mrs. Wong?

What if I hadn't accepted Iris's invitation to visit Beijing?

What if I'd shrugged off Leslie's suggestion of doing a full-day training?

What if the voice in my head won each conversation, and I'd only said "no"?

Here's what happened. Back home in Sheffield, I did my research and planning, then drafted everything I needed for my brand-new one-day workshop "Powerful Business Writing Skills". Iris and I communicated regularly, and she recommended that her boss, Mrs. Wong, should organise my first public programme. A few months later, I went back to Singapore and delivered my first one-day public training programme.

I must admit it was scary doing the first run, but I put together everything I'd learned over years of studying, teaching, and writing books. The result? A highly successful programme that has become a very popular choice among my clients.

Needless to say, one successful public programme evolved into many more and was soon extended to two days. Each year that followed, I designed and delivered more programmes. Soon I was receiving enquiries from organisations for in-house corporate training. Now my annual visits weren't only for pleasure. I could build my business, develop new relationships, and have a good time doing it!

"Character first. Title second.
Lead yourself first,
because no one else will."

– Michelle Ray

Reflections from Michelle Ray

Originally from Australia, Michelle Ray began her career in media and advertising, and she achieved outstanding results as a business leader. On a holiday in Canada, she toured the country and quickly fell in love with it. She went back to Australia and started visualising the life and job she wanted in Canada. Four years later, she got the opportunity she had visualised, and she emigrated to Vancouver.

Michelle Ray, international leadership keynote speaker, entrepreneur and author

But the real moment of truth came for Michelle when she started work. Although she'd taken a job she wanted, it didn't resemble anything like the same organisation she'd worked with in Australia. Its leadership was radically different. This proved to be the catalyst that led to Michelle leaving the company and setting up her own business. She is now a highly respected international leadership keynote speaker, author, and educator who teaches the importance of developing leadership and accountability skills, regardless of one's title.

> Leadership starts with *you!* We can all choose to be leaders of our own lives.

In her book *Lead Yourself First*, Michelle advocates that leadership starts with *you*. Rather than being all about a title on a door or business card, leadership is more about who you are, your character, what people remember about you, and how you interact with people. She believes all of us can choose to be leaders of our own lives or take charge of any situation, personal or professional. And when you're authentic and transparent, real and honest, these make up attractive traits in a leader.

In her work as a speaker now, Michelle addresses personal challenges that people often come up against. One is the "imposter syndrome" – not being confident enough or believing in oneself enough to step up. Indeed, if Michelle had listened to the inner voice that told her, "No, you can't do this. You can't leave Australia," she would never have moved to Canada and created the wonderful life she enjoys today.

Michelle told me a story about when she addressed the senior leadership of the police force in Canada, the RCMP. The organisation's newly appointed commissioner would be present, plus commanding officers and directors from around the country. Facing this challenge, she had moments when her inner voice said, "What are you doing speaking to all these people?" But she turned around the nerves by telling herself, "What an exciting opportunity this is. They chose me for a reason. They knew they could learn from me."

That day, Michelle had an amazing experience, soaked in this incredible honour, and her speaking career has been crazy ever since.

Reflections from Connecting the Dots.
Watch exclusive interviews with all
Shirley's guests.

The imposter syndrome and you

If you ever hear a voice in your head questioning whether you are worthy or doing the right thing, remember this: *You are not alone.*

I've heard this voice many times while writing this book. "Who wants to read your story?" "You're just Shirley from Sheffield." "You're not special." And many successful people – from CEOs to million-dollar speakers to powerful politicians – also hear that voice. Many people wonder if what we're doing is good enough, or if we'll soon be found out for being imposters.

The impostor syndrome is a feeling of being consumed with self-doubt and fear. A dark cloud hangs over your head, waiting to show you up as a fraud. Your internal voice taunts you. A debilitating voice drains your confidence; it puts you down, questions your accomplishments, and makes you wonder if it's worth taking a chance.

But think about this. If we listen to that inner voice, life isn't much fun. It could stop us from exploring new opportunities, experiencing new things. Chapter 2 talked about staying in our comfort zones. If we stay there too long, that comfort zone soon becomes uncomfortable, because everyone else will have moved on. With safety comes loneliness, weakness, and often regret.

Let's forget that voice in your head to see the reality of the situation depicted by this image:

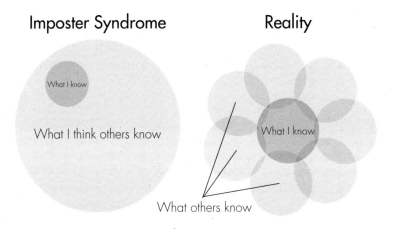

So, is there a cure for the impostor syndrome? I think the only cure is self-love. When you hear that voice saying, "You're not good enough, qualified enough, smart enough, beautiful enough," how will you answer? When you answer with kindness, compassion, and self-love, everything changes.

> The cure for the imposter syndrome is self-love and kindness.

We live in a world of comparing ourselves with others. Social media lays everything bare for the world to see. Or does it? The truth is, our timelines only show the best parts, the highlights. In reality, most of us are not as flawless and polished as we like to portray.

What if we simply accept ourselves as imperfect? What if we admit to our friends how we are feeling in bad times? They'll probably admit they often feel the same way. You will love each other no matter what – in fact, probably even more. That's the power of love, especially self-love.

It's time to change your script. You are *worthy*. You are *smarter* than you think. You are *better* than you think. You *know more* than you give yourself credit for. You are here for a reason. Remember this and remind yourself often!

8 steps to help you overcome the imposter syndrome

1. Acknowledge your feelings.
Too many people don't allow themselves to acknowledge they're having feelings of weakness, inadequacy. And if you hold these feelings in, they will fester. When you can acknowledge your feelings, you will be more open to handling things differently.

2. **Talk to someone.**
   Talk to a close friend, a family member, a coach or a therapist about your feelings. When you open up and realise you're not alone, it can be extremely freeing, and it may help you to get to the source.

3. **Stop comparing.**
   Every time you compare yourself to others, you will find some fault to fuel the feeling of not being good enough or not belonging. It may seem that others are achieving success effortlessly, yet even the most successful people face challenges. Stop comparing and start valuing your own strengths.

4. **Change the script.**
   Most people have a mental recording that starts playing in situations that trigger feelings of being an imposter. When you start a different job or sign a new contract, you might hear it: "They'll soon find out I have no idea what I'm doing." Instead of this, say to yourself: "I may not have all the answers, but I know I can find out."

5. **Give yourself credit.**
   Don't always wait until you receive outside validation of a job well done. There's nothing wrong with patting yourself on the back, and we all need to do this at times.

6. **Stop beating yourself up.**
   Most people make mistakes. So instead of beating yourself up for being human, forgive yourself, identify the learning you can take from what happened, and move on.

   "Failure is only the opportunity to begin again more intelligently."
   – Henry Ford

7. **Visualise success.**
Professional athletes do this all the time. You can do it, too. Spend time visualising yourself doing a great job at your next career interview or presenting at your monthly meeting.

8. **Fake it 'til you make it.**
According to Amy Cuddy in her famous TED talk, it turns out that "faking it" could actually help you "become it". If you wait until you're totally confident in doing something, you may never do it. Courage comes from taking risks.

My friend Alison gave me some great advice that I think of often. When I was particularly nervous about a presentation, she said, "Do you know what confidence looks like?" Of course, I said yes, and I knew exactly what I had to do. I've given myself that pep talk many times since. Thanks, Alison.

"There are still days when I wake up feeling like a fraud, not sure I should be where I am."

– Sheryl Sandberg

Your reflections

1. Write down your experiences with that voice in your head.

2. How do you feel when you hear that voice?

3. What has that voice ever stopped you from doing?

4. How have you moved on when you heard the voice?

5. What steps will you start taking to overcome feelings of being an imposter?

6. Complete this sentence. "If I truly believed I was good enough, I would…".

"The only way
to stop feeling like
an imposter is
to stop thinking
like an imposter."

– Valerie Young,
The Imposter Syndrome

A SMILE COSTS NOTHING

Staying positive through difficulties

"Once you replace negative thoughts with positive ones, you'll start having positive results."

– Willie Nelson

When I moved into a new rental apartment many moons ago, I invited a group of old friends to come over. Showing a few of the early arrivals around my new place, one of them (let's call her Celia) said, "It's so small." I replied, "Well, I have two bedrooms, and I'm the only person who lives here."

When I showed them the kitchen, Celia commented, "Gosh, it's tiny." To that, I replied with a smile, "It's perfect for me." Then of course came the big question. "How much is the rent?" When I told them, Celia said, "Good Lord. So expensive." I came back with, "Well, it's really close to Holland Village, and check out the great swimming pool."

When a few more people arrived, another friend, Martin, said, "Hey, it's quite spacious, isn't it?" and then, "Great little kitchen, just perfect for you." When I told him the monthly rent, he said, "Well, it's a prime area, so that's not bad."

People like Celia are draining to be around. When they walk in the room, you know you're in for a rant about anything and everything. This negative energy affects everyone around them.

Do you know a Celia or a Martin? Which one do you prefer to be around?

* * *

Singapore calls me back

During the '90s, I made many trips back to Singapore, and I started thinking it might make sense to set up a home and business there. My good friend Douglas said I could stay with him until I found an apartment to rent, so all I had to do was discuss this plan with Mum.

Mum had been on her own since Dad passed in 1987. She was grateful that a year before he passed, they had moved together to a bungalow, which they both loved. When I first went back home in the early '90s, I noticed Mum was struggling more than usual with her weight. She had a lot of difficulty walking even the shortest distances, and whenever we went shopping or for a trip to a country village, she often had to sit down because of her sciatica and other pains.

It was difficult to talk to Mum about this because she always took a very defensive attitude. But one day, I decided to take matters into my own hands. I had gained weight over recent years, too, so I started researching Weight Watchers. After gathering a lot of information, not to mention courage, I sat down and told Mum I wanted to speak to her about us both going on a diet. She held up her hand and said she was busy watching television. "That's okay," I replied. "I'll just sit here and wait until your programme's finished." She could tell I was determined and her delay tactics wouldn't work. After clicking off the power on the remote control, she heaved a heavy sigh and sat back, waiting for me to speak.

Mum was not at all happy about my suggestion, saying it would never work. So I approached it from a different angle, telling her, "Well, I'm going to join Weight Watchers, Mum, and it would be great if you would support me." Her response? She agreed to go to our first Weight Watchers meeting the following day. I'm pretty sure she didn't sleep much that night, and she was still not happy after lunch the next day as we drove to the meeting place.

Our Weight Watchers' leader Debbie was fun and friendly. She delivered a great meeting, using lots of visual aids and getting everyone involved. During her session, we heard from members who had lost 10 pounds, 20 pounds, even some more than 100 pounds. Mum was flabbergasted, but of course she couldn't imagine it happening to her. Debbie handed out materials and support, and Mum and I both laughed when she said, "I'll look forward to seeing less of you both next week!"

We followed the programme religiously, and we were both surprised how much food we were allowed to eat. At our second meeting, we were shocked when Debbie said Mum had lost seven pounds and I had lost four pounds. Seriously? How could that happen when we'd eaten so much?

And so began a whole new chapter in our lives, and a whole new relationship between me and my Mum. I became the head chef in the house, following all the fabulous recipes in our new cookbooks, **Working together really works.** and surprising Mum day after day with new meals. We would chart our daily progress together on our meal plans, and laugh when we felt we were eating better than ever before. After about six months, I was thrilled to have lost 35 pounds, and I reached my goal weight. Mum's weight loss took longer, but I supported her every step of the way. I was never more proud of her than when she reached her goal weight after shedding a grand total of 95 pounds!

Mum was a new woman. Wearing trousers for the first time, she looked and felt younger than ever. And guess what? Her sciatica was gone, replaced with a new energy and a new lease of life.

***

While I lived at home with Mum during that decade, our whole relationship changed. We enjoyed walking around the neighbourhood together, even with a neighbour's dog, and I enjoyed driving us both to country villages for pub lunches and a stroll around the shops. What a special time.

And, of course, Mum supported me with all my work for the LCCI Examinations Board. In fact, when I became an examiner, my Mum did, too. And when I became chief examiner, she became one of the examiners

The roles reverse for me and Mum.

on my team. Oh, how the roles had reversed. From Mum teaching me to me teaching her. From me doing homework for Mum years earlier to her marking papers for me to approve. At certain times, our house was full of examination papers and a lot of laughter. *And* a lot of love.

"In the middle of difficulty lies opportunity."

– Albert Einstein

Mum had certainly supported and encouraged me in all my trips to Singapore. She was always so proud of me, and she shared every new step and success of mine with everyone she knew. When I brought up the topic of moving back to Singapore in 2002, Mum was in her mid-70s. Sadly, after a knee replacement surgery went horribly wrong, she was no longer as mobile as she had been. Home health care workers visited three times a day to support her. So you can imagine the guilt I felt when I told her I'd like to move to Singapore again. Yet I always knew what Mum's reaction would be. She would never let anything become a reason *not* to continue supporting and encouraging me.

✳ ✳ ✳

In 2002, I returned to Singapore, found a great apartment, and set up my business there. Over the next few years, I grew my network and my business. I ran public programmes in business writing, email writing, and communication skills, as well as doing a lot of corporate training. But all the time, I kept in constant touch with my Mum. I phoned her almost every other day, and I went back every year, sometimes more than once, to check up on her. The carers were looking after her well, and she was as comfortable as possible.

Then one day in 2006, I got the call I was dreading. Mum had fallen and was in hospital. I dropped everything and flew home immediately.

Since Mum's knee surgery had turned sour, with all its consequences, we had previously discussed that she may need to go into a nursing home one day. Whenever the subject was raised, her reaction had always been the same: "You may as well shoot me!" This time, however, it was different. The doctors told me Mum would not be able to go back to her own home; she needed round-the-clock care. Mum was devastated.

I was lucky to find a place at a nursing home close to Mum's bungalow. The room was stark, with just a bed, side table, chest of drawers, and nothing on the walls. I knew I couldn't let Mum stay in a room like this, so I arranged to bring some of her furniture from home. Her favourite chair and wall unit, framed family photographs on the walls, the Chinese cabinet that she loved, containing all the small crystals I'd gifted her over the years, plus her own bedding and quilt covers, and a vase with her favourite artificial yellow orchids that I'd brought her from Singapore.

After giving her room a good clean and polish, the day arrived for Mum to see it. Oh, let me add that I'd kept all this secret from her. I'll never forget the day when Mum was pushed into the room in a wheelchair. With her head bent over, she looked thoroughly miserable. Then as she looked in her room for the first time, she straightened up, raised her head, and stared around in disbelief with her eyes and mouth wide open. The biggest smile came on her face while happy tears streamed down her face.

The care at the nursing home was excellent, with the staff giving Mum a lot of support. It wasn't easy for her, but she did settle down to knowing her life would continue within those four walls. But still, she wouldn't hear of me not going back to Singapore. Our phone calls increased to every day, and instead of annual visits, I flew home four times in the last two years of her life. Without going into detail about that time, suffice to say no one should have to suffer the pain, indignity, and embarrassment that Mum had to go through. Yes, she struggled, and she cried more than I'd ever known her cry in her life.

One day will always stand out for me. Mum knew two good friends would be visiting her that afternoon. She hadn't had a great day, and I asked if she wanted me to call and tell them not to come. Mum wouldn't hear of it. Just before they were due to arrive, she asked for her powder compact and lipstick, and she combed her hair, too. When Lily and Alan were with her, Mum was alert, smiling, and talking as much as she could.

Out of the blue, Lily said, "Eileen, how come you can put a smile on your face when you are in such pain and struggling so much?" My Mum smiled back and said, "Well, no one would come and see me if I was miserable."

"A smile is the best makeup any girl can wear."

– Marilyn Monroe

My Mum

Shirley and Mum on her 70th birthday.

LESSON:

A smile costs nothing.
No one wants to
see you if you're
miserable.

What if...?

What if Mum and I had lived in the same house but led separate lives?

What if I hadn't made it work with Mum on our weight loss project?

What if we'd found more negatives than positives in the programme we followed?

What if I hadn't made Mum's nursing home room look familiar by bringing her personal belongings?

What if Mum hadn't tried to look on the bright side despite her unfortunate circumstances?

Another memorable visit to Mum at the nursing home occurred on what was to be her last Christmas. I'd taken her good friend and neighbour, Marjorie, to see her that morning. When Marjorie took out her camera, I remember saying, "Oh, Marjorie, Mum is in such pain. I don't think she'll want to have her photo taken,"

Photo of me and Mum on her last Christmas D

I was wrong. Mum asked me to pass her powder compact and lipstick. Once again, she put a smile on her face. That would be the last photograph I'd ever have taken with my Mum. And I am forever grateful to Marjorie for that!

I was by her side holding her hands in July 2005 when my beautiful Mum passed away just a couple of weeks before what would have been her 80th birthday. I look at this photograph often, especially when I'm feeling down, to remind myself of her beautiful smile. And it always makes me smile too!

"The greatest discovery of all time is that a person can change his future by merely changing his attitude."

– Oprah Winfrey

Reflections from Andy Barrow

Andy Barrow grew up with a passion for sport. In 1997, he was playing rugby for his local club when he suffered a spinal cord injury that left him paralysed from the chest down, with limited use of his hands. He was only 17 years old.

Following this life-changing injury and many hard months of rehabilitation, Andy's life was transformed again when he discovered wheelchair rugby, also known as Murderball.

Andy Barrow, retired Great Britain wheelchair rugby player, Paralympic athlete.

Andy's wheelchair rugby career encompassed three Paralympic Games, three World Championships, and five European Championships, where he was part of a record-breaking team that won three gold medals in a row. He captained Great Britain's team from 2005 to 2010. One of his proudest moments was when he led his teammates out at the Beijing Paralympics in 2008.

When I asked Andy how he coped after such a tragic injury, he told me, "The injury was a freak accident, and of course, it was a really tough time, but a few days after the accident, a conversation in the hospital changed my life."

A nurse had come into his quarters, pulled back the curtains, and said, "Andy, I need to speak to you. I've heard you've been talking about walking out of here." Andy told him the doctors had mentioned there was a slim chance he would make a full recovery. The nurse then said, "Look, Andy, I need to tell you something. The doctors say that just to cover themselves, but there's no chance of you making a full recovery. There's no chance of you even making a partial recovery. You're not ever going to walk again. Never. Do you understand?"

When the nurse left, Andy sobbed and sobbed. He told me, "That was the worst moment ever, the lowest point in my life. But when I look back, I'm always thankful to that nurse, because it hit me that no matter how much I cried, there was nothing I could do to turn back the clock."

That incident flipped a switch in Andy's head. It made him see the full perspective of his situation. As he told me, "Instead of dwelling on what happened and thinking about things I *can't* control, I told myself to focus on the things I *can* control."

Completing his rehab was the most significant thing for Andy at that time. He spent a long time working to gain independence. When he discovered wheelchair rugby, he found it was not just a great emotional crutch that helped him heal, build confidence, and get physically fit. It was also a place where he found a great community. And so began his record-breaking career.

In 2012, 15 years after his tragic accident, the London Olympic and Paralympic Games was the greatest sporting event in Great Britain's history, and the perfect opportunity for Andy to end his rugby career on a high. After more than 100 appearances for his country, Andy decided to make that event his final tournament.

Since retiring, Andy has worked as a professional speaker, delivering motivational keynotes for audiences around the world on the theme of performance and teamwork. His ability to overcome adversity and then use that experience to become an international athlete gave him powerful insights into what it takes to achieve success.

He now runs his own company providing workshops, training, and seminars on themes of performance and diversity. He also uses his skills as a professional speaker to teach current UK Sport-funded athletes how to create maximum impact during their public appearances.

In 2018, Andy turned his attention to access. His experience as a world traveller gives him the credibility to work as a consultant with multiple aviation and rail organisations to improve the assisted travel process for customers with impairments.

On the volunteer side, Andy is a trustee on the board of directors for Great Britain Wheelchair Rugby and volunteering/care navigation charity IMAGO, as well as being a Laureus "Sport for Good" ambassador.

Reflections from Connecting the Dots.
Watch exclusive interviews with all
Shirley's guests.

"Everyone has the qualities
they need to be the best they
can be, but nothing will change
unless you change it."

– Andy Barrow

The power of positive thinking and you

Positive thinking is about more than having a cheerful, upbeat attitude. Positive thoughts can actually create real benefits in our lives that last longer than a smile.

Things do change when you smile.

Of course, that's not always easy. I don't wake up every day with a smile on my face, and sometimes it's hard to force it. But I know I feel better when I do, and very often things change when I smile.

What about you? Do you believe that happier people are more successful in life? Can positive thinking boost your health, improve your work and your skills? Can you increase your chance of success by changing your negative thoughts into positive images or feelings?

By studying successful individuals, top athletes, leading business executives, award-winning entrepreneurs, even great parents, it seems they all agree about the power of the mind and attitude. Basically, the actions you take, the energy you project, and therefore the results you achieve are infinitely different when you have a positive rather than a negative attitude. You have just read about this in Andy's amazing story.

Think back to the story about my Mum and me and our Weight Watchers journey. Mum was grumpy and negative at first, but the more we helped each other, the more positive we became, the more successful we were, the happier we were, and the more fun we had.

I recently read that research has found people who are more positive may be better protected against the damage caused by stress. Studies also show that hope and positivity help people make better health and life decisions, and that negative emotions can weaken immune responses.

So, in the words of Monty Python, how can we look on the bright side of life? Really, anything that makes you feel joy, contentment, or happiness will do the trick. I'm sure you can think of things that work well for you. Perhaps it's playing the piano, or joining your friends for karaoke. Perhaps it's painting, or taking long walks in the countryside.

Here are a few things that always work for me:

1. **Smile more.**
   Researchers have found that smiling – even fake smiling – reduces one's heart rate and blood pressure during stressful situations. When I feel low, all I have to do is look at funny cat videos on YouTube, and that instantly makes me smile and laugh. So, when you sense a black shadow overhead, try whatever YouTube humour therapy works for you.

2. **Reframe.**
   When you're sitting on the train and hear an announcement about a delay, your first reaction may be to stress and scowl. You worry about the meeting you'll miss or the work that's waiting. Instead, sit back, breathe, and reframe. Let's face it, there's nothing you can do about the train delay. Appreciate that you now have extra time to listen to podcasts, music, or news you've missed, or even study that report you've been meaning to review.

3. **Meditate.**
   Many studies show that people who meditate daily display more positive emotions than those who don't. They also build valuable long-term skills – for example, increased mindfulness, purpose in life, social support, and decreased symptoms of illness. There are many apps that help me meditate, even some that help me sleep better. When I miss a few days (okay, even weeks), I always benefit from revisiting this useful practice.

4. Play.

In our calendars, we schedule time for meetings, conference calls, regular events, and other responsibilities. What about scheduling time to play? How about blocking time just to have fun? Is being happy and content more important than your Thursday meeting? Sometimes, we don't give ourselves permission to do fun things by setting aside time to play. But when we do, we immediately feel the benefits of smiling, enjoying life, and feeling positive emotions.

Where to start? Well, positive thinking is not just a soft, fluffy, feel-good term. Moments of happiness and positivity are essential to opening our minds and building the skills that can be valuable in many other areas of life.

To put it simply, seek joy, play often, smile more, and pursue adventure. Your brain will do the rest.

"The way to happiness:
Keep your heart free from hate,
your mind from worry.
Live simply, expect little,
give much. Scatter sunshine,
forget self, think of others.

Try this for a week,
and you will be surprised."

– Norman Vincent Peale,
The Power of Positive Thinking

Your reflections

1. Do you see yourself generally as more positive or more negative?

2. How does this affect your life and your relationships with others?

3. What's a specific example of someone doing something with a positive attitude and energy that really impressed you?

4. What compliments have you given or received recently?

5. What could you be grateful for and positive about right now if you wanted?

6. What's one problem you're grateful you don't have?

7. What excuses do you need to let go of that might improve your life?

8. What area of your life might profoundly shift if you focused more attention on your positive attitude?

"The mind is everything. What you think you become."

– Buddha

PLANT SOME SEEDS

Success is about growing others

9

"Find a group of people who challenge and inspire you, spend a lot of time with them, and it will change your life."

– Amy Poehler

Evan is quite introverted, but he's always been interested to find out more about the business networking association that meets every month. He plucked up courage to go along to a meeting.

There was a refreshments and greetings session for half an hour before the meeting began, but Evan felt nervous because he didn't know anyone. He chose to sit at a table on his own and check out Facebook until the presentations began. Some other people sat at the same table, and they tried to make conversation. Evan answered their questions but then nervously turned his attention back to his phone. During the mid-session break, a couple of people said hello to Evan, and tried their best to make him feel welcome.

Evan attended the meetings several months in a row, but he didn't really get to know anyone, always keeping himself to himself. Some members who recognised him tried to get to know him, but Evan made little conversation.

Eventually, Evan stopped showing up at the meetings. He decided it was not for him.

What would you have done differently? Why?

* * *

I found my tribe

In 2005, when I'd been back in Singapore for a few years, a training colleague, Ricky, told me about Asia Professional Speakers Singapore (APSS). Ricky invited me to join him at their meeting that evening. I'd been a trainer for over two decades by then, and I'd done public and corporate training programmes around Singapore and Malaysia. But a meeting of professional speakers? Seriously? Me?

Ricky insisted I go with him. When I walked in the room, I felt totally intimidated as I saw groups of people talking together all over the room. I knew no one. Neither did Ricky, but that didn't stop him from approaching people to say hello and shake hands. Now, I'm actually an introvert by nature, but I'm fine once I get to know people. Some would say I'm rather outgoing. But I stuck to Ricky like glue that first evening.

I must have enjoyed the presentation. I decided to go back the following month, and the following, and I ended up becoming a member of the association. The more meetings I attended, the more I learned. The more I learned, the more I grew, both myself and my business. It wasn't long before I realised I'd found my tribe. I'm so grateful to Ricky for inviting me to join him that first fateful evening.

Over the years, I gained more friends through APSS than I could have imagined. By this time, I'd set up my own private limited company, STTS Training Pte Ltd, and I saw how working with APSS friends could be a win-win. Soon, STTS gained a solid reputation for quality training by professional speakers and trainers. We started providing corporate training not only in Singapore but throughout Southeast Asia. But little did I realise the universe had bigger plans for me to work with many of these trainers doing more than training.

***

Over lunch one day, my good friends and publishers Leslie Lim and David Buckland presented me with a new opportunity. They had both moved to a different Singapore publishing company, Marshall Cavendish International. They told me there was a strong market for a series of small books on personal development topics. David suggested they publish them under the STTS Success Skills series, with me being the series editor.

Once again, the universe had worked its magic and delivered a fantastic opportunity. This time, I could work with several members of my new tribe of speaker/trainer friends. I certainly wasn't short of experts I could invite to join this series. Over the next few years, we published a total of nine books in the STTS Success Skills series, many of them authored by friends who had never written books before. Before long, the publishers asked me to be editor again for a collaborative book featuring the contributions of nine colleagues. This very popular book is titled *Success 365: Great Ideas for Personal Development and Achieving Greater Success.*

> Once again, the universe works its magic, delivering a fantastic opportunity.

When this series took off, the same publishers came to me with yet another opportunity. "Hey, Shirley, you know lots of speakers and trainers in Singapore, so how about getting 22 of them to contribute one chapter each to a book?" By now, I'd learned to laugh when something like this happened. I had started going with the universal flow and realising these opportunities were sent for a reason – further professional and personal growth.

Of course, being editor and working with 22 people to write a book brought its own challenges, but eventually *88 Essential Secrets: For Achieving Greater Success at Work* was published, with the royalties assigned to APSS.

***

At one of our association's monthly meetings, David Lim, past president of APSS, came up to me and said, "Shirley, you should think about joining the executive committee. You'd make a good president one day." Well, talk about "knock me over with a feather" (as my Dad would say). It had never even crossed my mind! But then I asked myself, "What did David see in me that gave him confidence that I could be a leader in this association?" Whatever it was, he had planted the seed. I decided I would find out more.

In 2009, I joined the executive committee as secretary (of course!) and the following year became vice president. During that year, my good friend and president Tim Wade and I were fortunate to attend a training programme in Phoenix, Arizona, at the national headquarters of the National Speakers Association (NSA). Every year, NSA would hold this event for upcoming leaders of all its US chapters and also welcomed leaders from other international associations.

What an eye-opening event it was in Phoenix! I relished every moment, and I made friends I cherish to this day. But more than that, I enjoyed an amazing experience in leadership and service.

Over the course of only a few days, I watched and learned from many great leaders. I was inspired and encouraged by members who were serving their association for no financial gain – just for the pure pleasure of serving. I saw the benefits that could be gained when leaders support and encourage others, when they shine a light that helps others shine, and when they nurture the leaders of the future. There, I saw at first-hand what happens when great leaders plant seeds that help others to grow.

"Help young people. Help small guys. Because small guys will be big. Young people will have the seeds you bury in their minds, and when they grow up, they will change the world."

– Jack Ma

David Lim

David Lim with my cat Cookie.

LESSON:

We rise by lifting others.

What if...?

What if I'd stayed home instead of going to that first APSS meeting with Ricky?

What if I'd not attended the meetings regularly?

What if I'd not tried to get to know lots of other members?

What if I hadn't taken the opportunity to work with the publishers?

What if I'd discounted David's suggestion that I could be a great future president?

What if I didn't go to Phoenix for that training?

It was at the event in Phoenix that I learned about the Spirit of Cavett, which is really about the spirit of service, the spirit of giving. This was a story I hadn't heard before, but one that resonated with me — a story I would tell multiple times at conferences around the world. I hope you also find it inspiring.

"Before you are a leader, success is all about growing yourself. When you become a leader, success is all about growing others."

– Jack Welch

Reflections from the late Cavett Robert (1907–1997)

Cavett Robert had many careers, including being a salesman and lawyer, but because his fear of public speaking was holding him back, he took courses to improve this skill and overcome his fear. He also joined Toastmasters, and in 1942 on his second attempt, he won the organisation's International World Championship of Public Speaking.

Cavett became passionate about public speaking, and he dreamed of a world in which speakers helped each other to be better. He set about convincing some of his Toastmaster friends to create a national speakers association. In those days, the concept of helping each other in such a competitive market was unthinkable, so Cavett received little support. In fact, his friends thought he was crazy, saying, "Why should we help other people to be better speakers? They would just steal our piece of the pie!" Cavett's response was always the same: "Let's just build a bigger pie." His moral code was this: "Sure, individually we've all got a small piece of the pie now. But if we all work together, imagine the opportunities that could come along. We can create a much bigger pie for all of us."

Cavett never lost faith in this idea. In 1973, he founded the National Speakers Association (NSA). He built the association on the concept that "There is nothing that cannot be accomplished when the right people are swept up in a worthy cause, divorced from who gets credit for what!"

Over the next 10 years, three other national associations followed Cavett's lead in the US — New Zealand, Canada, and Australia. Then along came another pioneer. Warren Evans became founding president of the Canadian Association of Professional Speakers (CAPS). Wanting to take Cavett's expanding pie idea to the rest of the world, Warren became the driving force behind setting up a global entity. It took more than a decade of working with other association leaders, refining the concept, and resolving issues. Finally, in July 1997, a proposal was passed to approve the formation of the International Federation For Professional Speakers (IFFPS).

The IFFPS was set up to provide a channel through which associations and their members could share and benefit from each other's knowledge, experience, and, most importantly, wisdom. In 2009, the name was changed to the Global Speakers Federation (GSF). At the time of this book's publication, 17 associations around the world are proud to be part of the GSF. Thanks to Cavett Robert and all who followed him, his "pie" has become global. Each association provides a place where people can share, grow, and nurture each other.

Cavett Robert was a man who reinvented himself often and left a legacy of a better world through encouraging others. I hope this story makes you reflect on how you might encourage others to learn, share, grow and nurture each other.

Reflections from Connecting the Dots.
Watch exclusive interviews with all
Shirley's guests.

"There is nothing that can't be accomplished when the right people are swept up in a worthy cause, divorced from who gets credit for what!"

– Cavett Robert

The secret to happiness is helping others

Thank you to Jenny Santi for giving me permission to include her article here. Jenny Santi is a philanthropy advisor and author of *The Giving Way to Happiness: Stories and Science Behind the Life-Changing Power of Giving* (Penguin Publishing Group, 2016).

There is a Chinese saying that goes: "If you want happiness for an hour, take a nap. If you want happiness for a day, go fishing. If you want happiness for a year, inherit a fortune. If you want happiness for a lifetime, help somebody." For centuries, the greatest thinkers have suggested the same thing: Happiness is found in helping others.

And so we learn early: It is better to give than to receive. The venerable aphorism is drummed into our heads from our first slice of a shared birthday cake. But is there a deeper truth behind the truism?

The resounding answer is yes. Scientific research provides compelling data to support the anecdotal evidence that giving is a powerful pathway to personal growth and lasting happiness. Through fMRI technology, we now know that giving activates the same parts of the brain that are stimulated by food and sex. Experiments show evidence that altruism is hardwired into the brain – and it's pleasurable. Helping others may just be the secret to living a life that is not only happier but also healthier, wealthier, more productive, and meaningful.

But it's important to remember that giving doesn't *always* feel great. The opposite could very well be true: Giving can make us feel depleted and taken advantage of. Here are some tips that will help you give not until it hurts, but until it feels great:

1. **Find your passion.**
   Your passion should be the foundation for your giving. It is not *how much* we give, but *how much love* we put into giving. It's only natural that we will care about this and not so much about that, and that's OK. It should not be simply a matter of choosing the right thing, but also a matter of choosing what is right for us.

2. **Give your time.**
   The gift of time is often more valuable to the receiver and more satisfying for the giver than the gift of money. We don't all have the same amount of money, but we all do have time on our hands, and can give some of this time to help others – whether that means we devote our lifetime to service, or just give a few hours each day or a few days a year.

3. **Give to organisations with transparent aims and results.**
   According to Harvard scientist Michael Norton, "Giving to a cause that specifies what they're going to do with your money leads to more happiness than giving to an umbrella cause where you're not so sure where your money is going."

4. **Find ways to integrate your interests and skills with the needs of others.**
   "Selfless giving, in the absence of self-preservation instincts, easily becomes overwhelming," says Adam Grant, author of *Give and Take*. It is important to be "otherish", which he defines as being willing to give more than you receive, but still keeping your own interests in sight.

5. **Be proactive, not reactive.**
   We have all felt the dread that comes from being cajoled into giving, such as when friends ask us to donate to their fundraisers. In these cases, we are more likely to give to avoid humiliation than out of generosity and concern. This type of giving doesn't lead to a warm glow; more likely it will lead to resentment. Instead we should set aside time, think about our options, and find the best charity for our values.

6. **Don't be guilt-tripped into giving.**
   I don't want to discourage people from giving to good causes just because that doesn't always cheer us up. If we gave only to get something back each time we gave, what a dreadful, opportunistic world this would be! Yet if we are feeling guilt-tripped into giving, chances are we will not be very committed over time to the cause.

The key is to find the approach that fits us. When we do, then the more we give, the more we stand to gain purpose, meaning, and happiness – all of the things that we look for in life but are so hard to find.

"Give your hands to serve,
and your hearts to love."

– Mother Teresa

Your reflections

1. Write down various occasions when you have given your time to a person or a cause. It might be helping someone in your office or neighbourhood or an outside cause or movement.

2. How did you feel when you did this?

3. Who do you know personally who could benefit from your time, money, or problem-solving skills?

4. What do you value in life? Perhaps it's having a home. If so, choose a charity dedicated to providing housing for people in need.

5. What issues do you deeply care about? Perhaps it's finding cures for specific diseases. If so, contribute time and money to related research organisations.

"We make a living
by what we get;
we make a life by
what we give."

– Winston Churchill

ON OUR OWN, WE CAN ONLY GET SO FAR

Together we can help each other to grow

10

"*People who are truly strong lift others up. People who are truly powerful bring others together.*"

– Michelle Obama

Priya is a quiet girl who gets to work on time and leaves on time. She works very hard and is good at what she does. Her boss doesn't fault what she does, but he is concerned that, apart from a couple of people in her immediate area, she doesn't make an effort to get to know others. He's mentioned this to her a few times, and she keeps saying she will try harder.

Her boss hears from Ravi in Marketing, who has been tasked with heading a committee to organise the company's annual dinner and dance. He suggests that Ravi asks Priya to join the committee. She is hesitant at first because she doesn't know others on the committee, but she agrees after she's encouraged by her boss to take on this new role.

Within a few weeks, Priya finds she has a lot in common with the other three committee members. Dawn is also shy, but together they bring each other out of their shells. The four team members start having lunch meetings and often go to the movies after work, too.

Not only can they later say the annual dinner and dance was a huge success, but all the committee members found new friends *and* a new lease of life. Priya now smiles more, voices her opinions in team meetings – quietly but assertively – and has become a popular member of the team. And guess what? Priya and Ravi are engaged and planning a wedding for next year.

✳✳✳

My tribe becomes global

For me, getting deeply involved in APSS was pivotal in finding my new purpose. What I didn't realise at first was that while I'd found a new local tribe in Singapore, within a few years, I would become part of a huge global tribe.

As you read in the previous chapter, APSS is one of 17 speaking associations around the world that are members of the Global Speakers Federation. Being a member of APSS provides many benefits, one of which is paying member rates at events and annual conventions – plus, of course, meeting, networking, and learning from members of other associations when they visit Singapore. We also have Facebook groups that let us keep in touch with people we don't see often. These groups not only keep friendships alive, they also provide a valuable source of information when we need guidance or advice.

Every few years, a Global Speakers Summit is held in a different country. I made a point of attending my first GSS in Amsterdam in 2011 and again in Vancouver in 2013 and New Zealand in 2018. Through attending international events like these as well as NSA's annual convention, held in

> When you do new things, meet new people, expand your comfort zone, you never know what it may lead to.

different cities in the United States, I got to know people from all over the world. And they got to know me. I loved these events. Not only did I gain a tremendous amount of learning, I also gained a lot of new friends. What I didn't realise at first was how this might lead to successful collaborations.

One person I met at numerous events was Scott Friedman. A past national president of NSA, Scott was also a member of Asia Professional Speakers Singapore, and he visited Singapore regularly so I got to know him well. Scott has always been a huge advocate of the spirit of service and collaboration.

***

Around 2012, I was sitting in my Singapore office one day when I received a phone call from an American speaker named Marjorie Brody. I'd not met Marjorie personally, but I had heard her name in the speaking circles. Marjorie told me Scott Friedman had given her my name. Her company, BRODY Professional Development, had been working with a large international organisation to conduct BRODY's communication and presentation skills programmes in various cities across the US and Europe. Marjorie was now looking for a training coordinator in Southeast Asia who could find trainers to conduct these BRODY programmes.

Wow! What a bolt from the blue! My first reaction was (again silently), "Good Lord. Can I really do this? How can I pull this off?" But by now I'd become a risk-taker; I'd gained more confidence over the years; I'd become more positive. So, I told Marjorie I'd love to work with her on this. But I was thrown when Marjorie added, "What about Australia? Do you know trainers there?" My mind immediately started whirling, thinking "Who do I know? Who could help? There has to be someone." At the time, I remember saying confidently, "Oh yes, there's a huge network of speakers and trainers there, so I'm pretty sure I can find people we need through my connections."

I'm happy to say that I'm still working with BRODY to this day, and I value the relationships I have built with Marjorie and the other people at the company. Over the years, I have never conducted one of their training programmes myself. Instead, I've coordinated with about 20 trainers in Malaysia, Singapore, China, Australia, India, and Europe who delivered BRODY programs.

Whenever I'm asked, "Do you know anyone in…?" my first thought is usually, "Crikey! Here we go again." But then I confidently reach out to my network, and so far, I've always been able to find someone for the job.

It's beneficial for me and STTS, for BRODY, and for the trainers themselves. A great example of win-win-win.

***

Fast forward to 2019. I received a call from BRODY's COO asking if I could help find a trainer for a client in India. But this was no ordinary training. They were looking for someone who was not only an expert in communication and presentation skills, but also someone who could conduct a train-the-trainer programme.

Immediately, the right person popped into my mind: Marianna Pascal. For almost a decade I'd worked with Marianna, as she conducted communication and presentation skills courses for my company STTS throughout Singapore and Southeast Asia.

Over a period of three months, Marianna put her heart and soul into this project, and I enjoyed supporting her progress as she liaised extensively with the US project manager. On three separate visits to India, Marianna worked with the client's local trainers to help them deliver BRODY's communication programme to their staff. The local trainers and the company in India were thrilled with the results, the managers at BRODY were delighted, and Marianna thoroughly enjoyed the project. Win-win-win.

See what can happen when you let the universe guide you – when you grab opportunities, when you say yes instead of no. Everyone gains.

***

This introduction by Scott to Marjorie is quite typical of what happens in the speaking world. When we make an effort to get to know colleagues all over the world, this sort of thing happens regularly.

"The life you change
may be your own."

– from Together We Can Change
The World's theme song

Scott Friedman

Scott Friedman and Shirley.

LESSON:

On our own, we can get so far. Together we grow.

What if...?

What if I'd stayed in my home country of Singapore and hadn't made connections?

What if I'd never travelled to these global conventions?

What if I'd not tried to make friends with people from other countries?

What if I hadn't made an effort to know Scott?

What if I'd panicked when I got the call from Marjorie Brody and showed no confidence in myself?

What if I'd not previously taken risks that had improved my confidence?

In the previous chapter, you read how we call this the 'Spirit of Cavett', after Cavett Robert, a man who left a legacy of a better world through encouraging others.

I mentioned earlier that Scott Friedman is a great example of this spirit of service or giving. Apart from speaking, Scott spends a lot of time travelling for his philanthropic projects. In 2008, Scott and his good friend Jana Stanfield founded Together We Can Change the World with the mission of empowering and educating less fortunate children and women.

Currently, TWCCTW (www.twcctw.org) supports over 20 causes in seven Southeast Asian countries, namely: Cambodia, Indonesia, Malaysia, Myanmar, Laos, the Philippines, and Thailand. Groups of speakers routinely travel to these countries to assess the outcomes of their efforts. They visit. They learn. They teach. They entertain. More importantly, they show others that people care by providing hope and help.

Reflections from Gina Romero

Gina often introduces herself as someone who has failed in business several times since the age of 16, not because she is proud of her mistakes but because she values failure as a catalyst for success. And she has certainly achieved success – so much so that she now dedicates her life to helping others succeed.

Gina's passion for entrepreneurship came from growing up in the UK with her mother who left the Philippines in the '70s to work abroad as a domestic worker.

Gina Romero, entrepreneur and ecosystem builder

Like many Filipinos, Gina's mum sent money back home to her family in the Philippines. Indeed, the majority of money in the Philippines has long been made overseas and sent back to the country.

Fast forward many years. Gina met her husband Bobby and together they set up a small IT business. At first, she had no real interest in technology, but it seems the universe had different plans for her.

For decades, Filipino women had been relegated to a select number of jobs. Gina had always wondered how she could help bridge the gender gap and create better solutions. She soon discovered the key was technology, and IT became a huge part of everything she does.

Gina's passion to help women led to starting Connected Women, an award-winning job-matching platform for women entrepreneurs and freelancers. This initiative helps busy professionals worldwide to get more done by connecting them to virtual assistants in the Philippines.

Connected Women has truly become a game-changer. Through technology, it is equipping Filipino women with the skills to take control of their careers without having to leave their homes and their families. It's also helping to bring financial earnings back into the country.

As Gina told me, "Connected Women resonates with women everywhere because we believe that location independence is a powerful enabler for women in every walk of life. As technology advances, we will have an entirely different way to share, connect, work, and learn. Connected Women wants to be at the forefront of this transformation.

"As an entrepreneur, I believe that professional development and training should be accessible to all women regardless of geographical location, race, education, and financial standing. At Connected

Women, we select the top ten per cent of applicants who qualify for our job-matching program. However, there's much potential to increase that number if we can give them access to the training they need to succeed in the competitive global talent industry.

"We don't want to leave any woman behind, so we are partnering with global companies that care about empowering women through digital literacy and connectivity. By providing technology training to women in the Philippines and globally, we can unleash the potential of untapped talent and create a surge in economic participation."

If the gender gap is to become a thing of the past, we need more people like Gina Romero and more initiatives like Connected Women. It would be great to see more women supporting, encouraging, collaborating, and empowering each other to realise our full potential. When one of us smashes that proverbial glass ceiling, we make room for more to do the same.

Reflections from Connecting the Dots.
Watch exclusive interviews with all
Shirley's guests.

"In the remote work economy, #ConnectedWomen win. And so do businesses that hire them."

– Gina Romero

Collaboration is key

If you're reading this book in sequence, you'll realise how much value I have always given to people and relationships. When I look back to my earliest job as a secretary, most people had small, individual, closed offices – very different from our world today. But even in those days, we worked as teams. We quickly got to know people in other departments; we went out with colleagues at lunch time and in evenings. These connections and relationships helped everyone rely on each other, which meant they could work better. Having a collaborative environment contributed to the success of the organisation as a whole.

Today, coworking spaces or shared office spaces can be found everywhere. They seem to be a great fit for entrepreneurs, freelancers, and small businesses whose goals align with what shared spaces offer. So, what makes these coworking spaces special? And can they offer lessons to be applied in traditional offices?

A team of researchers studied the effects of coworking on productivity and published some of their findings in the *Harvard Business Review*. They found that productivity was higher in coworking spaces and attitudes different from those in a traditional office. People in these spaces regularly mentioned feeling their work was more meaningful; they had more job control and flexibility; and (no surprise) they felt a strong sense of community.

People clearly thrive in environments that allow them to communicate and work together. It's interesting to note that today's organisations are rethinking their office design to include shared working spaces and hot desks, which are desks that any employee can use any time, rather than being allocated to a specific worker.

In my opinion, supporting a friendly, collaborative environment should be high on everyone's list. Without collaboration and teamwork, if people don't get along, projects and productivity may suffer.

So, whether you're a team member or a manager leading a team, it's as much *your* responsibility as it is everyone else's to help create a successful team.

6 ways to become an essential team member

1. **Play to your strengths.**

   Your strengths, skills, and abilities are the commodities you bring to your team. Identify them, and don't be afraid to share what you do best. Ideally, your team includes a number of people with varying strengths. When this happens, it becomes easier to compensate for any weaknesses.

2. **Be honest about your limitations.**

   Identifying and understanding your limitations will help you become a stronger, more valuable team member. When you know where they lie, you can take action to overcome them by, for example, attending training. Or you can ask other team members to help on issues that are not best suited to your abilities. Once you understand your limitations, you can learn to accept this help without feeling threatened. Essentially, that helps you become a better team player.

3. **Communicate clearly.**

   Communicating well is critical for any successful team. To get to a place of working together like a well-oiled machine, it's essential to have clear, concise lines of communication. To do your part, take steps to master three of the keys to successful communication: listen, paraphrase, and reflect.

- **Listen** actively to what those around you are saying. This means focusing intently on those who are speaking and consciously digesting what they say.

- **Paraphrase.** Once you feel you have an understanding of what has been said, repeat or accurately paraphrase the dialogue. This will help you make sure you have a full understanding of the instructions, ideas, concerns, or opinions being shared with you.

- **Reflect.** Thinking before you speak is essential. If you slow down enough to do this, you can make sure you say what you mean and mean what you say.

4. **Don't be afraid to delegate or share work.**
   While teams are designed to ensure projects or tasks are tackled efficiently and effectively, one or two members quite often carry the load. In the most highly functional teams, every member shares the workload and contributes to the team's overall success. That means tasks must be delegated appropriately based on members' strengths and weaknesses.

   > Every team member can contribute to the team's success.

5. **Don't try to grab the limelight.**
   In a well-functioning team, all members are stars. Just like in sports, it takes every member performing well to bring home a win. Keep this in mind as you focus on the task at hand and the role you play in making it happen. The limelight will shine on the entire team – you included – if the assigned tasks are handled with expertise.

6. Don't shy away from teambuilding events.
Learning to work as part of a successful team rarely happens overnight. It can take time to build trust and an instinctive understanding of each other's strengths and weaknesses. This is where teambuilding exercises and events can come into play. While these exercises can seem silly on the surface, they pay off by helping everyone form a cohesive working bond.

When every individual learns how to work for the good of the team, everyone wins. The process starts with you.

"Coming together is a beginning. Keeping together is progress. Working together is success."

– Henry Ford

Your reflections

1. What are your strengths? Write down what you believe your strengths are, even if you think they go unnoticed.

2. Now list the strengths you think people see in you – what others believe you're good at, even if you disagree.

3. What are your limitations? List them.

4. What actions could you take to overcome those limitations?

5. What teambuilding exercises have been effective for you? In addition, what events or trainings have helped you?

6. What ways of working have contributed to building bonds at work? Outside of work?

"I can do things
you cannot,
you can do things
I cannot;
together we
can do
great things."

– Mother Teresa

IF EVERYONE LOVES YOU, YOU'RE DOING SOMETHING WRONG!

Leading with heart

"With integrity, you have nothing to fear, since you have nothing to hide. With integrity, you will do the right thing, so you will have no guilt."

– Zig Ziglar

If you were asked to give three responses to this question, what would your answers be?

What are the most important attributes in any leader?

For each of your three responses, ask yourself why. And then ask yourself which one you would put at the top of your list.

Here are some of the attributes that may be on your list: intelligence, competence, vision, accountability, competence, empathy, humility, integrity, resilience, vision, resourceful, positivity, communication skills, confidence.

So, what's your number one? For me, it would have to be integrity. It doesn't matter how capable, intelligent or resourceful a leader is. If a leader is involved in unethical behaviour, it will most likely lead to their undoing.

A person of integrity is bound by solid morals. They inspire and motivate others through ethical behaviour. To me, integrity is the most important attribute of leadership, because no matter how many other valuable qualities they have, people will not follow someone unless they know they can trust them.

For me, this is the essence of what I call leading with heart.

***

From local president to global president

In previous chapters, you read how significant it was for me when I moved to Singapore and found my tribe. Being a part of Asia Professional Speakers Singapore (APSS) helped me in multiple ways. I made dozens of friends, and from those friendships, I found trainers I could collaborate with by organising public workshops for them. Through APSS, a smaller group of friends set up a mastermind group that met every month to share our challenges and discuss projects. Through my connections with publishers, I was also able to work with many trainers as they wrote books for my Success Skills series.

Getting involved with the APSS leadership team proved to be a great learning experience, and becoming president was the ultimate honour. I worked hard during that year, coordinating with strong people on the executive committee as we organised valuable monthly meetings and numerous other events for our association members. I thoroughly enjoyed my year at the helm.

What I wasn't ready for, however, were the emails – the *critical* emails. It seems when you're in a position of power and responsibility, a lot of people think they know better than you. They often want to tell you what you should do differently.

Since childhood, I've found it hard to take criticism, which enhanced my inferiority complex and imposter syndrome. When I was the last one to be chosen on a team at school, it always hurt. If a teacher scolded me in front of others, I'd take it to heart. I've always disliked confrontation, preferring peace every time. For example, you'd never see me on the school's debating team. But if I have to stick up for a friend, then I'm right there at the front of the line.

Being ruled by my heart rather than my head, you can imagine how that first long, critical email cut me to the quick. And then another and another. I seriously had to stop myself from doing what my first instinct told me to do – crawl under a table and cry. Instead,

I'd call a former president for advice, and while talking on the phone, I paced up and down my lounge. I am forever grateful for the support and encouragement I received from those leaders. And every time I received one of those emails, I took a deep breath and replied courteously. I certainly learned to grow thicker skin.

Of course, with age and experience comes more wisdom and the realisation that it's hard to please everyone. But this advice from my parents always came back to me: "If you can't say anything nice, then don't say anything at all." Oh, if only more people would live by that old adage!

"If you can't say anything nice, then don't say anything at all."

* * *

Watch out for people who might be planting seeds for you!

During my APSS presidential term, the Global Speakers Federation president visited Singapore, and over lunch one day, she said to me, "Shirley, I think you'd make a good GSF president in a few years. Will you consider joining our board?" Crikey! However, this critical statement planted a seed in my head, just as David's did some years earlier. I asked lots of key leaders for advice, and before long, I found myself on the board of this prestigious global team. With board members living all over the world, we attended our monthly meetings via Zoom video calls. Participants were all leaders or former leaders of their own speaking associations.

I'm not too proud to put up my hand and say that, when first attending these calls, the imposter syndrome crept in again. Working with such well-respected leaders from the speaking world felt intimidating for me. But eventually, I found my voice and earned my place on the team. I soon started joining in the discussions and taking ownership of projects.

I learned a lot from serving on this global team and from attending our in-person meetings once a year, always held in the US When I was appointed president of GSF in July 2017, I knew I was standing on the shoulders of giants. They were big shoes to fill.

Again, I was grateful for support from former GSF presidents, particularly one highly respected leader, Nabil Doss, from Canada. I feel blessed to have served my apprenticeship with Nabil, who was GSF president the year before me. Working closely with him, I watched the way he conducted meetings, the way he was firm and assertive when appropriate, always respectful and choosing his words carefully. I could not have had a better mentor to prepare me for my own term as president.

But during that year, nothing could have prepared me for something that was even worse than criticism. This time it was back-stabbing. Have you ever been close to someone who seemed to be a great friend, but then you found they had been criticising you behind your back or, even worse, telling lies about you! I'm sure you can imagine how much this hurts. Of course, at first you don't realise what's happening. It might take months for it all to come to light. That's what happened to me, and it was like a bolt from the blue.

I won't go into detail here, but I felt it was important to mention this because, as tough a time as it was, I learned the most important lesson from it. It's exactly what I mentioned in my opening to this chapter. The number one attribute that I feel is essential for any leader is integrity. A person of integrity is bound by solid morals. They inspire and motivate others through their own ethical behaviour. People want to follow leaders they can trust.

> **A leader with integrity is bound by solid morals. They inspire and motivate others through their own ethical behaviour.**

I call this leading with heart.

This is exactly the type of leader that Nabil was. He was there for me throughout my presidential year, through the good times and the challenges. He listened respectfully, and gave me excellent advice when I needed it. He was always courteous and respectful. We had a good laugh about many things too, which always helped. I'm very grateful to have learned a lot from him.

As the 2017–18 GSF president, I travelled and spoke at many association conventions in different countries. Brian Walter, president of the National Speakers Association in the US during that year, attended most of the same events with his wife Karen, and we all became great friends. Brian always wanted to learn more about me as we talked through challenges, hopes, and plans for the future. And boy, did we have some fun!

Shirley, Brian and Karen in Singapore

In many ways, I feel I scored the jackpot during my year of service for GSF. Being supported by these two genuine, authentic leaders helped me a lot.

* * *

Nabil Doss

Nabil Doss, GSF President 2016–17.

LESSON:

Lead from the heart. Be kind, be respectful, be authentic.

What if...?

What if I'd cracked when I received the first (or second or third) critical email?

What if I really had crawled under the table and cried after reading each one?

What if I hadn't applied the feedback and advice I received constructively?

What if I'd tried to do it all alone instead of reaching out to respected leaders?

What if I hadn't had such great mentors?

During my year as GSF president, I delivered a lot of keynote presentations at speaking association events around the world. In my session "Connecting the Dots to Success", I told how I went from secretary Shirley in Sheffield to president of the Global Speakers Federation. I shared key turning points in my life and lessons I learned at each stage of my journey.

Feeling pleased with the response my presentation received, I was even more thrilled to get positive feedback. As you may have guessed, that keynote has morphed into this book, *Connecting the Dots to Inspire the Leader in You.*

I'm grateful to a highly respected speaker and friend, James Taylor, who, after seeing my presentation, sent me an encouraging email. It said: "Shirley, you have amazing skills to inspire, entertain and educate your audience, and your presentation showed you have a real heart. You connect on a very emotional level with your audience, with huge humanity."

To me, this is the ultimate praise. James cited the qualities I aim to show the world, not just as a speaker but as a leader. Thank you, James.

 Find out more here about my Connecting the Dots live or virtual presentation

Reflections from Andrea Edwards

In our changing world, new rules and new opportunities happen all the time. This is good, because Andrea Edwards has never been one to play by the rules. Her mission is to help everyone understand that if you own your voice, you own your future.

Andrea Edwards, The Digital Conversationalist

Andrea is a strong advocate of social leadership, content marketing, and employee advocacy. She helps businesses understand how they can empower employees to delight customers, grow personal career opportunities, and build brand success.

How? By leading with heart, with authenticity, and with integrity.

Gone are the days when people wanted to interact with brands. Today, humans want to interact with other human beings. Andrea advocates that organisations encourage leaders and all employees to share their stories and their authentic selves on social media. In doing so, Andrea says, "This will help them not just reach their own customers but also reach a company's multiple audiences – current employees, future employees, partners, influencers, stakeholders, shareholders, and more. The benefits can be incredibly powerful."

But how? Andrea suggests you start building your courage muscle. Just like any other muscle, the more you work on it, the more courageous you will become. You have to put yourself out there, get out of your comfort zone, stand up for what you believe in, find your voice, share your passion.

She told me about a senior leader who wrote an article on LinkedIn about his son who had become a great musician with a successful career in Los Angeles. The message he put out was that his son had eclipsed him and he wants anyone who

> Being vulnerable is powerful and can reap great rewards.

works for him to eclipse him, too. Guess what? Five customers called and wanted to meet him – all because he opened up by telling his story. Being vulnerable is powerful, and, as in this case, it can reap great rewards.

While encouraging executives to become social leaders and the voice of their companies, it's also essential to achieve the right balance. The best leaders are able to get their voice heard without sounding egotistical. This requires having a mindset of service while at the same time being humble.

So, think about how you can apply Andrea's advice. What personal story can you link back to and make it a professional story? How can you add a related message about the way you work? What can you share from your heart? How can you show your authenticity? What are you passionate about? It may be mentorship, women in leadership, mindfulness, health and welfare, or maybe blockchain, cloud, or artificial intelligence. *Talk about what you care about.* This will open the door to what other authentic leaders care about, too.

Andrea also strongly encourages leaders to engage with at least one employee a week on social media. When leaders publicly praise something their employees do, it has a massive impact. When you share an employee's content or write a comment on their posts, it not only boosts their self-esteem, it helps them be more successful – and will make you more successful, too.

"Don't be scared to lead with your heart. We are all here to sprinkle our own piece of personal magic on the world, in our own way, at our own time. When we have the courage to live our life leading from the heart, we then understand the mighty power of human potential, starting with our own potential first."

– Andrea Edwards

It's extremely important to be authentic, real, genuine. Essentially, you've got to be *you*. And don't worry about perfecting the message itself. That's old school, and it's not relevant anymore. When you are not authentic, even if it's just a whisper, people can hear it. Audience members today quickly switch on when they hear genuine voices. Why is that important? Because when you are authentic, you build trust.

Andrea says: "Digital platforms are screaming out for genuine voices and for professionals to lead from this service mindset. So, let's not hide who we are. Embrace this amazing opportunity to be 'real' in a world that often feels plastic. As we explore the many opportunities in this digital age, together we can shape the future of business and humanity."

 Reflections from Connecting the Dots. Watch exclusive interviews with all Shirley's guests.

Leading with heart

For me, the ultimate quality a good leader needs in abundance is the one thing that holds our world together – trust. Stephen Covey said that trust is the glue of life, the foundational principle that holds all relationships. Without trust in any relationship, there will be alienation, conflict, division, and much more.

There are many behaviours that will destroy trust and alienate your followers. Here are my top five:

1. **Lack of integrity**
    There are many things you may lack and still manage quite well. Integrity isn't one of them. Great leaders will have solid ethics and incorporate them into everything they do. They will

communicate those ethics to all their followers and walk their talk by living them. If you lack integrity, it will be found out and come back to haunt you.

2. **Excessive ego**
   As my Dad would say, this is being the big "I am". Great leaders leave their egos at the door. They supress their own personal agendas for the greater good of the organisation. Doing this requires a lot of self-awareness and honesty about personal motivation.

3. **Withholding information**
   There's a huge connection between distrust and information that's withheld. When leaders don't share information, followers feel they are not trusted. Unless there's a good reason not to share something, keep all stakeholders informed with open communication.

4. **Showing anger**
   Uncontrolled anger has no place in leadership. Anger conveys fear, disrespect, lack of control, and no concern for those who are on the receiving end. Stress is inevitable, and so are challenges and errors. But don't push your frustrations on your staff or colleagues. Find a mentor or a support group where you can share them and work out how to deal with them.

5. **Lack of humility**
   So many people are impressed with leaders who have a powerful, charismatic personality and an impressive presence. I believe we should look deeper and admire leaders who have a quiet confidence and a sincere focus on others. Humble leaders know how to get the most from people. When things go wrong, they acknowledge their mistakes and take responsibility for them. And when things go right, they shine the spotlight on others.

5 building blocks of trust

You can really feel a difference when you work with leaders who create high levels of trust. A person can talk about the importance of trust until they are blue in the face, but they will never *build* trust unless they walk their talk and show it every day.

Here are five building blocks of trust that you must have if you want to be an authentic leader:

1. **Transparency**

    People are apprehensive about unknowns. If they hear rumours or are not informed about something, they will probably assume the worst. If leaders meet in secret or show some people favouritism over others, it will be hard for others to trust them. Team members thrive when leaders keep everyone informed.

2. **Sincerity**

    People can usually sense when leaders are insincere or inauthentic. As a result, it's hard to believe anything they say. For example, it's hard to believe someone who stresses the importance of communication if they love the sound of their own voice. Sincerity is a quality that draws people in, strengthening engagement and contribution.

3. **Congruency**

    Acting congruently means making sure *what you say* matches *what you do*, and vice versa. It also means matching your values to your actions, and vice versa. At the core of congruence is honesty. Without being honest with yourself, you can't be truly honest with others. And don't think people won't notice, because they will. No one wants to work for a boss who gives lip service to something, but doesn't follow up with meaningful action. Some people may think they can get away with contradictions, but others will quickly detect a lack of congruency.

4. **Vulnerability**

   Leaders who never admit mistakes rarely get the truth from others. If a leader gets something wrong, then admits it and apologises for it, he or she will usually get others to do the same. If they don't own it in this way, others may not feel comfortable sharing their thoughts or disagreeing with them. If you want a powerful tool to build trust (or rebuild lost trust), take ownership of your mistakes and apologise for them.

5. **Reliability**

   People inherently value reliability. We need a reliable car, reliable Wi-Fi, reliable phone coverage, reliable transport. We also need leaders who do what they say they will do. A leader who is true to their word and fulfils their commitments will encourage trust. Being reliable gives people peace of mind, strengthens relationships, and ultimately helps everyone deliver better results.

> **"Trust is the glue of life.
> It's the most essential ingredient
> in effective communication.
> It's the foundational principle
> that holds all relationships."**
>
> **– Stephen R. Covey**

Your reflections

1. Write down the name of someone you know or admire who is a great leader.

2. What admirable qualities would you say this person has?

3. With digital platforms screaming out for genuine voices, how can you extend your reach with authenticity in your current social media activity?

4. What additional digital platforms could you use to expand your reach to multiple audiences?

5. In your opinion, of these five behaviours that undermine trust – lack of integrity, excessive ego, withholding information, showing anger, lack of humility – which do you feel are the most destructive?

6. Of these five building blocks of trust – transparency, sincerity, congruency, vulnerability, reliability – which ones are your strongest? Weakest? What can you do to build them?

"To earn trust, money and power aren't enough; you have to show some concern for others. You can't buy trust in the supermarket."

– His Holiness the Dalai Lama

TIME TO MOVE ON

Leap and the net will appear

"In the process of letting go,
you will lose many things
from the past, but you will
find yourself."

– Deepak Chopra

What exactly does the phrase "let it go" mean? To me, it goes back to when I was nine years old in a deep-sea fishing boat off the east coast of England with my granddad and brother, when I let go of the fishing rod by accident. Everyone watched as the expensive rod floated away, never to be seen again. That was an *embarrassing* letting go.

I also remember helping my Mum make lunch, and I picked up what I didn't know was a hot saucepan with an oven glove. I let it go immediately because the glove had a hole in it. That was a *painful* letting go.

This chapter looks at the kind of letting go that involves a *conscious* letting go. This type can also be painful at times as well as challenging or scary.

Letting go in this sense means releasing all fear or reservations about a situation or an outcome. It means getting rid of anything that's making you unhappy or is no longer serving you. Letting go is a choice you make to stop focusing on what you *can't* control, and to deal with what you *can* control instead.

This type of letting go lets you say goodbye to yesterday. It closes some doors and enables new doors to open. And it creates space for fresh starts (like making room in your closet for new clothes by letting go of old ones) and new opportunities (like pursuing adventures in a different country).

Every day, you have choices. Will you keep holding on just a little longer? Or will you decide that *today is the day* you will finally let go?

* * *

The end of an era

Living in Singapore for so many years (18 at the time of publication of this book), I travelled a lot, often long distances. Usually, whenever I flew back to Singapore, just as we were landing I had this fuzzy feeling wash over me. "I'm home," it whispered contentedly. A few years ago, something happened that knocked me for six. Just as the plane was coming into land, the feeling washing over me shouted, "Why are you still living here?"

I was still reeling from the shock of this when I got in a taxi to head home, so I called one of my closest friends, Heather Hansen, and told her what had happened. Heather instantly said, "I know exactly what it means. There's nothing here that inspires you anymore." Wow! She'd hit the nail on the head. By that time, I'd lived in Singapore for almost 14 years. I'd grown a lot in that time – from being a one-woman band and charging peanuts for my training services to setting up my own training company with three employees and several freelance trainers.

This was truly a shock to my entire system.

***

Heather and I first met in 2007 at a conference in Singapore. A mutual friend (Ricky Lien, who took me to my first APSS meeting) had told Heather, "You need to meet Shirley." He also said the same thing to me, so we both looked out for each other at the conference. The moment we met, we hit it off. It was like we'd known each other for years. We've often joked that we must have been connected in many previous lives.

> "There's not a word yet for old friends who've just met."
> – Jim Henson

Despite a big age difference, Heather and I developed a close friendship over the years.

***

That experience hit me like a ton of bricks. I started asking myself if I was really happy in Singapore. Particularly in recent years, I'd relished the opportunities to travel and experience different cultures, make new friends, learn new things. I'd developed my network and established not only a local tribe but a global tribe. Was I now yearning for more, something that Singapore couldn't provide?

This really made me start thinking that it might be time for me to move on. But where? How?

Meanwhile, my life in Singapore carried on, business as usual. Singapore is a vibrant, lively metropolis, a clean, green, and safe country to live in. It's also hot and humid all year round, with a fast-paced lifestyle, and my life here very much revolved around work. Of course, I'd made good friends here, too, but Singapore is a transient country. Every few years, the good friends I'd made moved on. At this time in particular, it seemed that one friend after the other was moving back to their home countries or somewhere else. Even Heather and her family moved to Denmark in 2014 when her husband's business moved him back to his home country.

***

I explored various options. Should I move to Canada? The US? How about heading back to the UK? This dilemma tore me to pieces for quite some time, years in fact.

One of the biggest question marks hovered over what to do with my business. I'd built STTS Training Pte Ltd from scratch into a highly successful training business. We had key clients that we had worked with for years, providing communication training in countries all over Southeast Asia. I worked with several independent trainers who delivered programmes in presentation skills, communication skills, critical thinking, and more. All this plus of course my own popular communication skills, email and business writing programmes.

Business was good, especially in my own topics. I was also thankful that my books on communication skills and email and business writing had continued to sell well. And I was thrilled to see a big increase in the number of organisations realising the importance of training their staff in effective writing skills.

So, with business going so well, how could I just stop and drop all this? How could I leave it all behind? I struggled to find the answer. More than that, I felt stuck, like I was standing with my feet in mud and couldn't move at all. It was an awful feeling. Little did I know that the universe was about to work its magic again and bring me the answer.

* * *

In 2018, after living in Denmark for almost five years, life took another turn for Heather and her family when her husband Peter's job brought them back to Singapore. Having Heather close by again, she and I talked a lot about my situation over many months, tossing around all the options.

While having lunch at her house one day, Heather suddenly announced, "I have the answer for you, Shirley. Let me take on the sole licence to market and deliver your email and business writing programmes in Southeast Asia."

After a few seconds of sitting there in shock, with my mouth and eyes wide open, I jumped up, screamed, and then ran around her living room like a crazy woman. It had never even crossed my mind to consider this possibility! Yet I instantly knew this was the answer I needed.

Heather is a specialist in global English, speaking, pronunciation, people skills, and presentation skills. With her focus being on everything to do with oral communication and mine focusing on written communication, we shared the same philosophy about the importance of human connection.

This couldn't have been a more perfect match. I already knew Heather as being ambitious, forward-thinking, and an astute businesswoman. Now, she was giving me the opportunity to move out of Singapore while leaving my legacy behind.

It took many months of detailed planning and working with a lawyer to get an agreement in place. I'm happy to say that on 1 February 2020, Heather's company, Global Speech Academy, became the sole licensee of my proprietary email and business writing training programmes in Southeast Asia.

Shirley and Heather drinking a toast to their collaboration.

Heather Hansen

Shirley and Heather Hansen.

LESSON:

Some people
come into your life
to teach you how
to let go.

What if...?

What if I'd not kept my friendship with Heather over time and distance?

What if I'd continued on the treadmill of my life in a city I wanted to leave?

What if I'd not been open to discussing a licence agreement with Heather?

What if I hadn't been ultimately willing to let go of my own successful business?

From the time Heather and I sat down to lunch that fateful day, a lot of water has gone under the bridge. After feeling stuck for so long, slowly but surely things started getting unstuck. Interestingly, as soon as I accepted the fact that the UK was the right choice for me, everything started to change. Another pivotal point was putting a plan down on paper.

My plan was very simply what I would do in January, then February, then March, April, May. I included everything from microchipping my cat Coco Chanel, to getting quotes from removal companies, to meeting with accountants and corporate secretary, to clearing out cupboards and drawers, and advertising furniture for sale online. I also wrote down a specific date by which I would sell my apartment, the price I wanted to get for it, and another date when I wanted the sale to close.

In effect, this plan was a wish list. I couldn't be sure of anything, especially regarding the sale of my apartment at a precarious time. But guess what? *I sold my apartment in the month I wrote down, I got the price I wrote down, and we closed on the date I wrote down.*

Joseph Campbell's quote comes to mind here: "If you are on the right path, you will find that invisible hands are helping."

> "If you are on the right path, you will find that invisible hands are helping."
> – Joseph Campbell

But here's a question to ponder. Would everything have happened like this if I hadn't made a very conscious decision to let go?

Will everything go smoothly with my agreement with Heather? Will everything go well with my move to England? Who knows! Only time will tell. I'm ready to leap and find out.

"Every great move forward in your life begins with a leap of faith, a step into the unknown."

– Brian Tracy

Reflections from Chester Elton

I recently interviewed bestselling leadership author Chester Elton for my online summit. In chatting with him about change and moving on, Chester told me a wonderful story about his good friend, Darren.

Chester Elton, bestselling leadership author and workplace expert

Darren was a senior leader in a company he loved working for. The CEO was a great cheerleader and supporter of everything Darren did in the company. His philosophy was, "Go out and change the world." He supported the direction Darren wanted to take the company and gave him free rein, saying, "Take it wherever you want to go."

Darren flourished in this environment. He loved going to work, and he loved the team he led. The CEO was delighted with the results Darren and his team produced. Everyone was happy.

However, when the CEO retired, his replacement had a very different vision and mission for the company. It seemed that overnight, everything went from "change the world" to "protect our margins". After 15 years with the company, Darren was disappointed. He found the new CEO didn't support his division or its focus. Because Darren had given the company his blood, sweat, and tears for so long, he found it traumatic to realise there was no longer a fit. He did stay on with the company, however, with an attitude of, "Never mind, I'll just crack on and keep my head down and bring in as much business for the company as I can."

Around the time of his 25th wedding anniversary, Darren's wife pulled him aside and said, "Look, it's clear that you're miserable. I don't know what we'll do going forward, but I'm telling you this: We're not doing this anymore. *I want my husband back.*"

That was a huge wake-up call for Darren. For much of his time with the company, it was his dream job. There had been no luckier guy on the planet, until those last two years changed everything. Darren's wife made him realise that being miserable at work affected his entire life. He came home anxious and frustrated, and it affected everyone around him.

Darren decided he had to jump ship. For almost two decades, he'd had a secure job, with a high pay check plus an expense account, a travel account, and everything else that goes with it. Suddenly, he was out on his own, working for himself, and scared. Darren admits the transition wasn't easy; it was very stressful. But with his wife's support, he built his own business.

Now, a decade later, with his wife working beside him, their business is thriving. They travel the world together with their work; they feel they are making a difference; and they've never been happier.

Reflections from Connecting the Dots.
Watch exclusive interviews with all
Shirley's guests.

"It's not the chances you did take that you regret. It's the chances you DIDN'T take that you regret the most."

– Chester Elton

10 lessons on letting go

I've had to let go many times in my life. Moving from Sheffield to Singapore in 1983 was a huge leap. Then to Bahrain and Toronto, Sheffield, and back to Singapore. We don't only have to let go of places, but also jobs, careers, and relationships.

Most of us are guilty of holding on at times. But holding on to pain doesn't fix or change anything, and neither does repeating the past over and over again. There comes a point when you have to accept that you're stuck or you're holding on to someone or something. It might be best to *just let go*. It's often the only way anything will change.

I don't claim to be an expert in this; I still have a lot to learn. But here are ten lessons about letting go that I didn't realise I'd learned at the time. The benefits of hindsight!

1. **Let go of thinking you can control others.**
    I learned this lesson from my great friend and mentor, Pam, in my early years overseas. I was wasting time and emotions wishing other people would change, but the truth is the only person we can change is ourselves. No one else will change unless and until they are good and ready, and they may never be. But we can change. We can change our mindset and our attitude. You can find great peace in accepting what is and letting go.

2. **Let go of disappointment when dealing with people.**
    Don't look for guarantees when you're dealing with others. You can believe you have the best relationship with friends for years, then something happens and, bam, they're gone. This can hurt – a lot. Creating respectful boundaries is something I wish I'd learned years ago. By setting the right boundaries, I could have avoided the pain of letting go.

3. **Let go of self-limiting beliefs.**
Too many people think, "Oh, I can't do that!" or "I'd be no good at that!" Why put these invisible chains around yourself when you have the key? It's simply to open your mind and believe in yourself. Know that when you take that first step, the second one will follow. Remember, we have to get out of the uncomfortable zone to move into the growth zone.

4. **Let go of worrying what others will think.**
It's easy to stifle progress with thoughts like, "I can't do that. What will people think?" If people criticise, so be it. You will never please everyone. Remember, if everyone loves you, you're doing something wrong. Live by your values, not for the approval of others.

If everyone loves you, you're doing something wrong.

5. **Let go of beating yourself up.**
Have you ever said something silly or done something stupid that you regret? I know I have. But that's okay. It makes us human. What's not okay is not to learn from it. When this sort of thing happens, reflect on the experience and do better next time.

6. **Let go of bottling up your emotions.**
People aren't mind readers. If you don't tell them how you feel or what you think, how can they know? Tell the people in your life what works and what doesn't work for you. It helps no one if you bottle up your emotions.

7. **Let go of dwelling on the past.**
What's the point in wishing things were the way they once were? What's the point of thinking, "If only I'd..."? *Right now* is where life happens. You *can't* change the past, but you *can* make decisions today that will define what happens in your future.

8. **Let go of fear.**
   Most fears fill us with doubt and worries that can imprison us. Fear can keep you stuck in your comfort zone. Fear will stop you doing many things that could help you change your future. The more you step out of your comfort zone, the more risks you take, the less fear you will feel, and the more confidence you'll develop. Do something that scares you today!

9. **Let go of grudges.**
   If you hold on to resentment, you will never move forward in your life. In fact, you will likely become bitter. Even though it may be hard to forgive someone, you probably won't be able to move on until you do it. By forgiving, remember, you aren't doing it for another person. You're doing it for yourself. Just forgive and let go. In its place, you will find peace.

10. **Let go of being too serious.**
   Life is hard enough without being too serious. I learned this from my parents. Look for the fun in the smallest things. Relax and enjoy the journey. I am constantly recalling something my Mum or Dad would have said to lighten up a situation. No need to be too serious. Laugh at yourself. Have fun. Smile more.

> **"When I let go of what I am, I become what I might be."**
>
> – Lao Tzu

Your reflections

1. What are you holding on to that you know you have to let go of?

2. What's the worst that could happen if you did let it go?

3. What's the best thing that could happen if you actually let it go?

4. Write down a list of actions you'd need to take to make this happen. Make a week-by-week or month-by-month list to get you started.

5. "Don't waste your time and energy trying to change someone, for the only person you can change is you." Who in your life might you be trying to change? What can you do to move forward?

"Faith is taking the first step, even when you don't see the full staircase."

– Martin Luther King, Jr

CONNECTING THE DOTS

The Common Thread

"You can't connect the dots looking forward; you can only connect them looking backwards. So you have to trust that the dots will somehow connect in your future."

– Steve Jobs

You've now read the stories about my journey along the road of life, as I've shared key turning points and lessons learned along the way. Did any of my stories help you see areas in your own life where you might be stuck? Did the stories from my guest contributors hit a nerve about something you need to change? Did you have any "aha" moments that made you stop and think? Did you find it helpful reflecting and writing down your thoughts? Perhaps they highlighted key areas where you need to shake up your life, reframe any fears, and recognise how you can recreate your future.

So, now it's time for me to connect the dots. As you were reading, could you see the common thread throughout all my stories and turning points? Have you already figured out what it is?

When I present my keynote "Connecting the Dots" around the world, audience members often suggest that the common thread is a constant need to step out of my comfort zone. Well, yes, that's certainly true. At every stage of my journey, I did have to step out of my comfort zone. Or maybe I was just expanding my comfort zone little by little, pushing back the boundaries. So, yes, that's definitely been an essential part of my journey. However, we need to find the *ultimate* common thread that connects every "dot".

To help us connect the dots, let's first look again at all my "dots" and the lessons I've learned.

✳ ✳ ✳

Heather Hansen
Some people come into your
life to teach you how to let go

12

Nabil Doss
Lead from the heart.
Be kind, respectful
and authentic.

11

Scott Friedman
On our own, we can
get so far. Together
we grow.

10

David Lim
We rise by lifting others.

9

My Mum
A smile costs nothing.
No one wants to see you
if you're miserable.

8

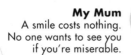

Leslie Lim
It's time to change the
narrative. You are worthy!

7

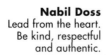

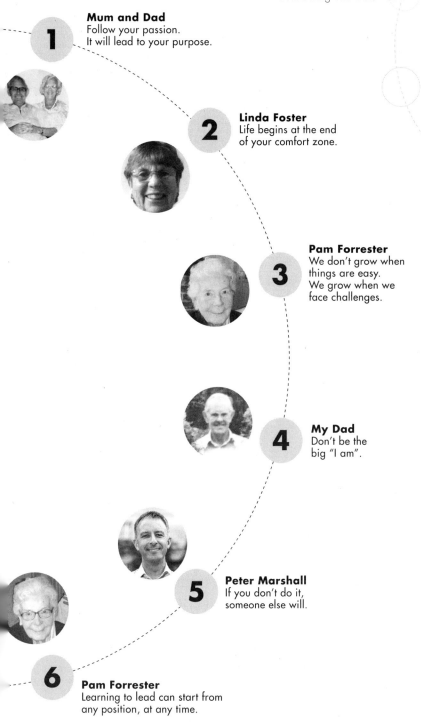

Mum and Dad
Follow your passion.
It will lead to your purpose.

Linda Foster
Life begins at the end
of your comfort zone.

Pam Forrester
We don't grow when
things are easy.
We grow when we
face challenges.

My Dad
Don't be the
big "I am".

Peter Marshall
If you don't do it,
someone else will.

Pam Forrester
Learning to lead can start from
any position, at any time.

THE COMMON THREAD

When I look back, I see clearly that the common thread at each stage of my journey was a person – a key relationship with a human being. I believe that building relationships is the most important thing we can do today. And I don't say that in a way that means exploiting relationships for different purposes. Absolutely not.

Let's look at Pam Forrester, for example. Just because she helped me when I first moved to Singapore, it didn't mean I would drop our friendship when I moved on. Pam was an important influence and mentor for me when I moved to Singapore. Of course, I wanted to keep her in my life. She visited me in Bahrain when I moved there. She visited me and my family when I moved back to Sheffield. I visited her at her home near London whenever I came to the UK. I loved Pam like a second mother.

Let's look at Leslie Lim. He was so influential when I started writing books, arranging for talks in bookstores, taking me around colleges to meet teachers and students. Every time I came back to Singapore, we met up for coffee or lunch, and we became good friends. He always had ideas for other books that I might consider writing. And guess what? After completing my year as GSF president, Leslie was the person who took me out for coffee and said, "Shirley, enough books on business writing. When are you going to write the Shirley Taylor story?" And so began *Connecting the Dots to Inspire the Leader in You.*

Let's look at Heather Hansen. You read earlier about how we felt we'd known each other for years the moment we first met. When Heather moved to Denmark, we kept in touch regularly. And when I needed a bolt hole – somewhere to hide and heal after my precious cat Cookie died – Heather told me to get on a plane to Denmark.

Being around Heather, her family, and her two cats certainly helped me to heal. Have we ever had challenges in our friendship? Of course, as with most friendships, there have been bumps in the road. But with time, reflection, and talking, we got our friendship back on track stronger than ever.

Interestingly, I had planned on finishing this book about six months before I did, but something always got in the way. Looking back, I realise I couldn't have finished it earlier. I needed to wait until I had wrapped up the Singapore leg of my life's journey. As you read in Chapter 12, Heather was hugely influential in that.

"Friendship is the hardest thing in the world to explain. It's not something you learn in school. But if you haven't learned the meaning of friendship, you really haven't learned anything."

– Muhammad Ali

Never underestimate the value of people

Looking back at my writing journey as I've drafted this book, in the beginning I never thought about including other people's stories and turning points. But as I progressed, I had some "aha" moments. When writing the chapter on passion, I thought of Moustafa Hamwi. When writing the chapter on comfort zones, my friend Nishant Kasibhatla came to mind. When writing the chapter about everyone being a leader, I thought about the author, Mark Sanborn, who I'd met through Dot #10, Scott Friedman, and my connection with the global speaking world. When I needed input on the topic of authenticity, my friend Andrea Edwards was top of mind. And so it goes on.

Was I nervous when I reached out to these people (and all the others) to ask if I could include their stories in this book? Absolutely, I was. But not one of them said no. In fact, everyone said they were honoured, even flattered, to be asked and included.

Building relationships is powerful

As I write this closing section, I am on a plane heading to the UK to begin my new life there. Waiting for me at Heathrow Airport will be Sue and Steve, who I will stay with for a few weeks. I met Sue almost three decades ago when I recruited her for a job in Singapore. After she moved back to the UK, we kept in touch. When I lived in Sheffield in the '90s, Sue and Steve often drove up to stay with me. Every time I've been back to the UK, my name has been on their guest room door. They have become two very dear friends – and two more connected dots!

Relationships – the ultimate common thread

I strongly believe there are more "dots" I have yet to meet – people who will have a huge influence in my life. But for now, as a Singapore Airlines plane flies me back to Blighty, I am looking out of the window filled with an assortment of emotions. I think back to something I wrote in Chapter 5:

> The stimuli for feeling nervous often include a racing heart, sweaty palms, and visualising an unknown future. What are the stimuli for excitement? A racing heart, sweaty palms, and visualising the unknown future.

And that's happening to me right now. As I think of my unknown future, my heart is racing, and my palms are sweaty. Am I nervous? Yes, for sure. I'm also excited. Very excited. Beginning this new chapter on my life's journey, I can only hope I will follow all the advice I've shared with you in this book.

Mostly, though, I hope my stories, my guests' stories, and all the lessons and learning points will inspire you in many ways – to navigate change, to unlock potential, to adopt a positive outlook during challenging times, and to create new opportunities for growth.

And if you're not sure where you want to go right now, I hope this book will help you to look inside, reflect, and figure it out. I hope reading this book helps you find the courage, the positivity, and the confidence to do something about any uncertainty so you can let your light shine brightly.

Remember, no matter where you are today, you *can* change your narrative. And when you do, it will shift your state of mind and ultimately change the outcomes you experience.

I wish you much joy in connecting your own "dots" to great success!

Shirley Taylor

Do you want to see what happened to me after writing this book? Would you like to share your turning point stories?

I've set up a Facebook group called 'Shirley Taylor Connecting the Dots'. I'll be updating it regularly, and including lots of inspiring and motivating content and interviews.

Please join the group. Let's learn, share and grow together.

 Shirley's Facebook group
'Shirley Taylor Connecting the Dots'

"Change will not come
if we wait for
some other person
or some other time.
We are the ones
we've been waiting for.
We are the change
that we seek."

– Barack Obama

ABOUT THE AUTHOR

Shirley Taylor discovered the challenges of communicating across cultures when she left her home in Sheffield, England, to teach in Singapore. There she began what became a passion for helping people to communicate more effectively.

Since then, Shirley has worked in the Middle East and Canada, and for 18 years she ran her own training company in Singapore. Her speaking and training work has taken her all over the world.

Shirley has established herself as a leading authority in email and business writing skills. She is author of 16 successful books, including international bestseller, *Model Business Letters, Emails and Other Business Documents* (seventh edition). This book has sold over half a million copies and been translated into 17 languages.

Shirley is now a trusted member of the global speaking community. She served as 2011–12 President of Asia Professional Speakers Singapore, and as 2017–18 President of the Global Speakers Federation.

Find out more about Shirley on her website, www.shirleytaylor.com

A MESSAGE FOR YOU

I hope the stories of my turning points, as well as those of my guests, have inspired you or impacted your life in some way.

It would be great to hear about any "aha" moments or changes you've made as a result of reading my book. I'd also love to hear about your turning points and your dots.

Your stories may inspire many others. So, please join my Facebook group and let's all help each other to grow and reach our true potential.

I'd love to hear from you.

Shirley

 Join my Facebook group
'Shirley Taylor Connecting the Dots'.

BOOK SHIRLEY FOR LIVE OR VIRTUAL PROGRAMS

I would love to work with you and your organisation. Here are some of my key programs:

- Connecting The Dots To Grow Yourself And Your Business
- Rock Your Role In Our Automated World
- It's 2020, not 1920. Are You Proving You're Human?
- Email Writing That Works
- Powerful Business Writing Skills

 Full details of all my programs are shown on my website. Please let me know how we can work together.